'Levi's first book, his account of Auschwitz, was called *If This is a Man*. After reading *Other People's Trades* you are inclined to say to yourself: "This is a man". There is nothing heavy or preachy about these delightful essays, but taken together they add up to a memorable portrait of what a human being is or ought to be' *Sunday Telegraph*

'A book to return to in the anticipation of pleasure of a bracing intellectual kind' *TLS*

'Read an essay or two every few days; it'll be like meeting him in a Turin café, hearing him talk of wonderful, funny and horrible things in his gentle, dry voice, with all the virtues of his chemist's training – "humility, patience and method", a wonderful nose and eye, and a steady hand'
*New Statesman & Society*

'Throughout *Other People's Trades,* by precept and example, Levi proclaims the great truth that the man with a writer's blood in him should be able to write well about anything. If he is bored, let him write about boredom; if he is ignorant, let him write about ignorance; and if he can write as capably as Primo Levi, then he is a man of rare and enviable gifts'
*Catholic Herald*

'Levi is essential reading for everybody, not least for the young, with whom he seems to have a direct rapport'
*Times Educational Supplement*

'A fine achievement, and a rare one' *Spectator*

'This is a wonderful book. It contains "maximum information with minimum clutter". The whole is absolutely greater than the sum of its parts' *Jewish Chronicle*

'Everything Primo Levi has ever written is well worth reading, and this collection is no exception' *The Times*

'A wonderful book – shows what a genius was lost to the literary world with the death of Levi' *Independent*

D0259835

*Also by Primo Levi in Abacus:*

# OTHER PEOPLE'S TRADES

## Primo Levi

*Translated by*
*Raymond Rosenthal*

AN ABACUS BOOK

First published in Great Britain
by Michael Joseph Ltd 1989
Paperback edition published by Abacus 1991
Reprinted 1992, 1993

Printed in England by Clays Ltd, St Ives plc

ISBN 0 349 10185 X

Abacus
A Division of
Little, Brown and Company (UK) Limited
165 Great Dover Street
London SE1 4YA

# Contents

# Contents

# Other People's Trades

If one lives in a compact, serried group, as bees and sheep do in the winter, there are advantages; one can defend oneself better from the cold and from attacks. But someone who lives at the margins of the group, or in fact isolated, has other advantages; he can leave when he wants to and can get a better view of the landscape. My destiny, helped by my choices, has kept me far from the agglomerations; too much a chemist and a chemist for too long to consider myself a real man of letters; yet too distracted by the vari-coloured, tragic or strange landscape to feel a chemist in every fibre. In short, I have travelled as a loner and have followed a winding path, forming for myself a haphazard culture; full of gaps, a smattering of knowledge. In recompense, I have enjoyed looking at the world from unusual angles, inventing, so to speak, the instrumentation: examining matters of technique with the eye of a literary man, and literature with the eye of a technician.

The essays collected here (which have already in large part been published in the Turin newspaper *La Stampa*) are the fruit of my roaming about as a curious dilettante for more than a decade. They are 'invasions of the field', incursions into other people's trades, poachings in private hunting preserves, forays into the boundless territories of zoology, astronomy, and linguistics: sciences which I have never studied systematically and which, for just this reason, affect me with the durable fascination of unsatisfied and unrequited loves, and excite my instincts as a voyeur and kibitzer. In other essays, I have dared to take positions on current problems, reread old and modern classics, or explore the transversal bonds which link the world of nature to that of culture; I have often set foot on the bridges which unite (or should unite) the scientific and literary cultures, stepping over a crevasse which has always seemed to me absurd. There are people who wring their hands and call it an abyss, but do nothing to fill it; there are also those who work to widen it, as if the scientist and literary man belong to two different human sub-species, reciprocally incomprehensible, fated to ignore each other and not engage in cross-fertilisation. This is an unnatural schism, unnecessary, harmful, the result of distant taboos and the Counter-Reformation, when they do not actually go back to a petty interpretation of the Biblical prohibition against eating a certain fruit. It did not concern Empedocles, Dante, Leonardo, Galileo, Descartes, Goethe and Einstein, the anonymous builders of the Gothic cathedrals and Michelangelo; nor does it concern the good craftsmen of today, or the physicists hesitating on the brink of the unknowable.

Sometimes I am asked with curiosity, or even arrogance, why I write though I am a chemist. I hope that these essays, within their modest limits of commitment and scope, will make it clear that between 'the two cultures' there is no incompatibility; contrary, there is, at times, when there is good will, mutual attraction. What's more, I hope I have conveyed to the reader an impression which I have often had: we are living in an epoch rife with problems and perils, but it is not boring.

Primo Levi
16 January, 1985

# OTHER PEOPLE'S TRADES

# My House

I have always lived (with involuntary interruptions) in the house where I was born; so my mode of living has not been the result of a choice. I believe that I represent an extreme case of the sedentary person, comparable to certain molluscs, for example limpets, which after a brief larval stage during which they swim about freely, attach themselves to a sea-rock, secrete an outer shell and stay put for the rest of their lives. This happens more often to people born in the country; for city people like myself it is undoubtedly a rare destiny, which involves peculiar advantages and disadvantages. Perhaps I owe to this static destiny the never satisfied love I harbour for travel, and the frequency that a journey appears as a *topos* in many of my books. Certainly, after sixty-six years on Corso Re Umberto, I find it difficult to imagine what it would mean to live, not just in another country or city but actually in another part of Turin.

My house is characterised by a lack of character. It resembles many other quasi-patrician houses of the turn of the century, built of brick just before the irresistible advent of concrete; it is almost bereft of decorations, if one excepts some timid memories of Liberty in the friezes above the windows and the wooden doors which open on the staircases. It is unadorned and functional, inexpressive and solid: it has proven this during the last war, when it went through the bombings, escaping with some slight damage to the window frames and a few scratches which it still bears with the pride that a veteran bears the scars left by his wounds. It has no ambitions, it is a machine for living, it possesses almost everything that is essential for living and almost nothing superfluous.

With this house, and with the apartments I live in, I have an unnoticed but profound relationship, such as one has with a person with whom one has lived for a long time; if it were torn down, and if as a result I moved to a more beautiful, more modern and more comfortable house, I would suffer like an exile, or like a plane tree which has been transplanted in soil to which it is not accustomed. I read somewhere the description of the one of the artifices of mnemonics, that is, the art (cultivated in the past by the learned and scholars and today foolishly abandoned) of exercising and improving the memory: whoever wants to remember a list of thirty, forty, or more names and then amaze his friends by reciting them even backwards, can achieve this if he makes a mental link (that is, invents any sort of connection) between each single name and, in an orderly sequence, a corner of his house; for example, proceeding from the front door to the right and exploring successively all the corners. Then, going over the same itinerary in the imagination, one can reconstruct the initial list; if one goes through the house in the opposite direction, one will also invert the direction of the list.

I have never had to carry out this performance, but I do not doubt that in general it works. However, it would not work in my case because in my memory all the corners of my house are occupied, and authentic memories would interfere with the chance, fictitious ones demanded by this technique. The corner to the right of the front door is the one which fifty years ago held an umbrella stand, and where my father, walking back from his office on rainy days, deposited a dripping wet umbrella, and on fine days his walking stick; and where for twenty years hung a horseshoe found by my uncle Corrado (at that time one could find horseshoes on Corso Re Umberto), an amulet about which it would be difficult to decide whether or not it had exerted its protective charm; and for another twenty years there hung from a nail a large key whose purpose everyone had forgotten but which nobody dared throw away. The next corner, between the wall and the walnut closet, was coveted as a hiding place when we played hide-and-seek; I had hidden there, on some unspecified Sunday of the Oligocene, and knelt down on a sliver of glass and still bear the scar on my left knee. Thirty years after me, my daughter hid there, but she laughed and was found immediately; and after another eight years my son, with a flock of his friends, one of whom lost a baby tooth in that very spot and for mysterious magical reasons shoved it into a hole in the plaster, where it probably still is.

Continuing along the right-hand path, one encounters the door of a room which looks out on the courtyard and which over the decades has had different uses. In my most distant memories it was the 'good' living-room, where my mother, two or three times a year, received important guests. Then for a number of years it was slept in by a fabulous 'live-in maid'; after that, it was my father's business office until, with the war, it was used as a bivouac and dormitory for relatives and friends whose houses had been wrecked by the bombs. After the war (and the end of requisitioning due to the Fascist racial laws) my two children have one after the other slept and played in it, and my wife has spent many nights in it, attending them when they were sick; I never did, with the iron-clad alibi of work at the factory and the Olympian selfishness of all husbands. At the moment it is a multiple laboratory where photos are developed, the sewing machine is operated, and amusing toys are constructed. Such transfigurations can be recounted for all the other rooms; a short while ago, and with some discomfort, I realised that my favourite armchair occupied the precise spot where, according to family tradition, I came into the world.

My house has a good location, not too far from the city's centre and yet relatively quiet; the proliferation of cars, which fills every cavity like compressed gas, has by now reached here, but only for a few months has it been hard to find a parking space. The walls are thick, and noises from the street are muffled. In the old days it was completely different; the city ended a few hundred metres to the south, people walked across the meadows 'to see the trains', which then, before they dug the trench system of the Zappata crossing, ran level with the ground. The roads on the outskirts were covered with asphalt only around 1935; before that they were paved with cobblestones, and in the morning we were awakened by the noises made by wagons coming from the countryside: the clatter of their iron rims on the cobblestones, the cracking whips, and the shouts of the drivers. Other familiar voices rose from the street at other times of the day: the cries of the glazier, the rag and junk man, the buyer of 'combed hairs', to whom the already mentioned 'live-in maid' periodically sold her hair which was long and grizzled: occasionally beggars played the barrel-organ or sang in the street, and we'd throw them some coins in a twist of paper.

Through all its transformations, the house I live in has preserved its anonymous and impersonal appearance; or, at least, so it seems to us who live in it, but it is well known that each of us is a bad judge of the things which concern us, of his own character, his virtues and vices, even his own voice and face; perhaps to others it could appear greatly symptomatic of my family's tendency to live apart. Certainly, at a conscious level, I have never asked of my house anything more than the satisfaction of elementary necessities: space, warmth, comfort, silence and privacy. Nor have I ever knowingly tried to make it mine, assimilate it to myself, embellish it, enrich it, refine it. It is not easy for me to speak about the relationship I have with it; perhaps it has a feline nature, like a cat I enjoy the comforts but I can also get along without them and could adapt myself pretty well even to uncomfortable lodgings, as has happened to me several times, and as happens each time I stay at a hotel. I do not think that my way of writing is marked by the environment in which I live and write, nor do I think that this environment can be seen in what I have written. So I must be less sensitive than the average person to the suggestions and influences of the environment, and not at all sensitive to the prestige which the environment confers, preserves or diminishes. I live in my house as I live inside my skin: I know more beautiful, more ample, more sturdy and more picturesque skins: but it would seem to me unnatural to exchange them for mine.

# Butterflies

The building, at present (1981) being remodelled, which housed the main hospital of Turin's San Giovanni Battista, is not a pleasant place. Its ancient walls and very high vaults seem imbued with the sufferings of generations; the busts of the benefactors, which flank the staircases, gaze at the visitor with the sightless eyes of mummies. But when one reaches the transepts, that is, the crossing of the two median naves, and the butterfly exhibit mounted there by the regional museum of natural history, one's heart expands, and one feels thrown back to the ephemeral and cheerful situation of a student on a school outing. As happens with all well-structured exhibits, indeed as happens any time one partakes of spiritual food, one leaves the exhibit nourished and at the same time hungrier than before.

If a hypothetical zoologist, who specialised in birds and mammals but knew nothing about insects, were told that there exist hundreds of thousands of animal species, very different from one another, who have invented a way of building themselves an armour by exploiting an original derivate from glucose and ammonia; and that when, in growing, these little animals must 'jump out of their skins', that is to say, out of this unextendable armour, they throw it away and make themselves another, larger one; that, in their brief life, they transform themselves, assuming shapes more different from one another than a hare from a carp; that they run, fly, jump and swim and have been able to adjust to almost all of the planet's environments; that in a brain weighing the fraction of a milligram they can store the crafts of the weaver, the ceramicist, the miner, the murderer by poison, the trapper and wet nurse; that they can feed on any organic substance, alive or dead, including those synthesised by man; that some of them live in extremely complex societies and practise food conservation, birth control, slavery, form alliances, make wars, engage in agriculture and cattle breeding; well, this improbable zoologist would refuse to believe it. He would say that the insect-model comes from science fiction: but that if it really existed it would be a terrible competitor for man, and would sooner or later overwhelm him.

In the world of insects, butterflies occupy a privileged position: anyone visiting a butterly exhibit realises that a similar initiative devoted to Diptera and Hymenoptera, even at the same level of scientific dignity, would be less successful. Why? Because butterflies are beautiful, but not only for this reason.

Why are butterflies beautiful? Certainly not for the pleasure of man as Darwin's opponents claimed: butterflies existed at least one hundred million years before the first man. I believe that our very concept of beauty, necessarily relative and cultural, has over the centuries patterned itself on them, as on the stars, the mountains, and the sea. We have proof of this if we consider what happens when we examine the head of a butterfly under the microscope; for the greater part of observers, admiration is replaced by horror or revulsion. In the absence of cultural habit, this new object disconcerts us; the enormous eyes without pupils, the antennae-like horns, the monstrous jug-like mouth, look to us like a diabolical mask, a distorted parody of the human face.

In our civilisation (but not in all) vivacious colours and symmetry are 'beautiful', and so butterflies are beautiful. Now, the butterfly is a real colour factory: it transforms into brilliant pigments the foods it absorbs and also its own excreta. Not only this: it knows how to obtain its splendid metallic and iridescent effects with pure physical means, simply by exploiting the effects of interference we observe in soap bubbles and the oily slicks that float on water.

But the butterfly's attractiveness derives not only from colours and symmetry: deeper motives contribute to it. We would not think them so beautiful if they did not fly, or if they flew straight and briskly like bees, or if they stung, or above all if they did not enact the perturbing mystery of metamorphosis: the latter assumes in our eyes the value of a badly decoded message, a symbol and a sign. It is not strange that a poet like Gozzano ('the friend of chrysalises'), passionately studied and loved butterflies: it is strange, however, that so few poets did love them, especially since the transition from caterpillar to chrysalis, and from this to butterfly projects alongside itself a long admonitory shadow.

Just as butterflies are beautiful by definition, indeed our yardstick for beauty, so caterpillars ('insects in default', as Dante called them), are by definition ugly: clumsy, slow, bumbling, voracious, hairy, obtuse, they are in turn symbolic, the symbol of what is crude, unfinished, an unattained perfection.

The two documentaries which accompany the exhibition show us, through the portentous eye of the movie camera, what very few human eyes have been able to see: the caterpillar which hangs in the aerial and temporary tomb of the cocoon, changes into the inert chrysalis, and then comes out into the light in the perfect shape of the butterfly; the wings are still inept, weak, like crumpled tissue paper, but in a few instants they strengthen, stretch and the newly born lifts in flight. It is a second birth, but at the same time it is a death: what has flown away is a psyche, a soul, and the ripped open cocoon, which is left on the ground, is the mortal remains. In the deep layers of our consciousness the butterfly with its restless flight is animula, faerie, sometimes even witch.

Its strange English name, butterfly, the fly of butter, evokes an ancient Nordic belief according to which the butterfly is the sprite that steals butter and milk, or makes them turn sour;

and the Acherontia Atropos, the large nocturnal moth, with the sign of the skull on its bodice which Guido Gozzano meets in the villa of Signorina Felicità, is a damned soul 'which brings sorrow'. The wings that popular iconography attributes to fairies are not the feathered wings of birds but the transparent and veined wings of a butterfly.

The furtive visit of a butterfly which Hermann Hesse described on the last page of his diary is an ambivalent annunciation, and has the flavour of a serene presage of death. The old writer and thinker in his hermitage on the Ticino sees rise in flight 'something dark, silent and phantom-like': it is a rare butterfly, an Antiopa with its brownish-purple wings, and it alights on his hand. 'Slowly, with the rhythm of calm breathing, the beauty opened and shut and opened its velvet wings, clinging to the back of my hand with six, hair-like legs; and after a short instant disappeared, without my realising its departure, in the great warm light.'

# News from the Sky

Immanuel Kant recognised two wonders in creation: the starry sky above his head, and the moral law within him. Let us leave aside the moral law: does it dwell in everyone? Is it true, can we accept the idea that it is congenital in us, is born with us, and in the course of a single life evolves and matures, or instead degenerates and is extinguished? Every passing year augments our doubts; faced by the political necrosis which afflicts our country, and not only ours; faced by the mindless nuclear armaments race, one cannot avoid the suspicion that over the moral law there prevails a perverse principle according to which power is acquired by those who for this law, which we feel to be unique in every time and place, the cement of all civilisations, have no use, do not feel its goad, are without it and do well without it.

The starry sky, however, remains: it is over everyone's head, even if we city people see it rarely, obfuscated by our fumes, narrow among the roofs, and offended by TV antennae. And in this regard, be it said in passing, a thought disturbs me: unlike radio waves, those used for television are not reflected downward from the high atmosphere; they are not enclosed in our terrestrial space, they are not a private matter of ours. Visible light behaves in the same way, for example, urban nocturnal lighting, but this contains only scant information: TV waves, on the other hand, are very rich in information, they penetrate the ionosphere and escape into cosmic space; the Earth, at those wavelengths, is 'luminous', is loquacious, and an acute extra-terrestrial observer, properly equipped and interested in our business, could learn much about our government crises, detergents, aperitifs, and baby's nappies. From all this he would derive a curious image of our way of life.

But let us return to the starry sky. When on serene nights we see it from some observatory distant from our disturbing lights, it is still the same: its spell is unchanged. 'The beautiful stars of the Bear' are the same ones that restored Leopardi's peace, the 'W' of the Cassiopeia, the cross of the Swan, gigantic Orion, Bootes' triangle flanked by the Crown and by the Pleiades dear to Sappho are still always the same; we learned to know them as children and they have accompanied us throughout life. It is the sky of the 'fixed stars', immutable, incorruptible; the antagonist of our terrestrial world, the noble–perfect–eternal which embraces and envelopes the ignoble–mutable–ephemeral.

But no, we are no longer allowed to look at the stars like this, in this naïve, reductive way. The sky of present-day man is no longer the same. We have learned to explore it with radio telescopes, and to send into orbit instruments capable of picking up the radiations which the atmosphere intercepts: now we are expected to know that the stars visible to our eyes, naked or assisted, are a tiny minority; the sky is being rapidly populated by a crowd of new, unsuspected objects.

One hundred years ago the universe was purely 'optic'; it was not very mysterious and it was thought it would grow less and less so. It appeared friendly and domestic: every star was a sun like ours, larger or smaller, warmer or less, but not heterogeneous; some in fact were a little restless, a few new stars had appeared, but everything led one to believe that the design of the universe was the same everywhere. The spectroscopes sent reassuring messages: nothing to fear, in the stars there was hydrogen, helium, magnesium, sodium, and iron, the raw materials of our home-grown chemists.

It was considered probable that every sun-star had its retinue of planets: some astronomers (first among them all, Camille

Flammarion, the indefatigable and enthusiastic populariser) actually asserted that it *must* have it, otherwise it would have no reason to exist. In fact, every planet, including those of our sun, must harbour life or must have done so, or must be destined to do so in the future: observers whose eyes were too sharp saw on the moon vapours and fleeting lights, and on Mars networks of canals too regular and geometric to be only the work of nature. A universe inhabited solely by us, who are so imperfect, would have been an immense, useless machine.

Now, the sky which hangs over our head is no longer domestic. It becomes ever more intricate, unforeseen, violent and strange; its mystery grows instead of decreasing, every discovery, every answer to old questions, gives birth to thousands of new questions. Copernicus and Galileo had wrenched humanity from the centre of creation: it was only a change of location, yet many felt deposed and humiliated by it. Today we realise much more: that the imagination of the artificer of the universe does not have our limits, indeed has no limits, and our astonishment also becomes limitless. Not only are we not at the centre of the cosmos, but we are alien to it: we are a singularity. The universe is strange for us, we are strange in the universe.

Generations of poets and lovers have looked at the stars with familiarity, as at the faces of close relations: they were friendly symbols, reassuring, dispensers of destinies, ever-present in popular and sublime poetry; with the word 'stars' Dante ended the last three verses of his poem. Today's stars, visible and invisible, have changed in nature. They are atomic furnaces. They do not transmit messages of peace or poetry to us, but quite other messages, ponderous and disquieting, decipherable to a few initiates, controversial, alien.

The birth rate of celestial monsters grows immeasurably greater; our everyday language fails to describe them, it is inept. There are 'small' stars of unimaginable density, which rotate tens of times per second shooting out into space since ever and forever, a radio babble without destination and without meaning. Other stars emanate energy with an intensity superior to our entire galaxy and so distant as to appear to us the same as they were at the beginning of time. Other stars yet are no warmer than a cup of tea; down to the too much talked about 'black holes', for the time being more the fruit of speculation than observation, presumed graves and celestial gullets, whose gravitational field is supposedly so strong that it lets neither matter nor radiation issue from it.

The scientist-poet is not yet born and perhaps never will be born who is able to extract harmony from this obscure tangle, make it compatible, comparable, assimilable to our traditional culture and to the experience of our puny five senses made to guide us within terrestrial horizons. This news from the sky is a challenge to our reason.

It is a challenge that must be accepted. Our nobility as thinking motes demands it: perhaps the sky will no longer be part of our poetic patrimony, but it will be, in fact already is, vital nourishment for thought. It is possible that our brain still is a 'unicum' in the universe: we do not know, nor will we probably ever know, but we now already know that it is an object more complex, more difficult to describe than a star or a planet. Let us not deny it alimentation, let us not yield to the panic of the unknown. Perhaps it will be up to them, the students of the stars, to tell us what we were not told, or told badly, by prophets and philosophers: who we are, where we come from, and where we are going.

The future of humanity is uncertain, even in the most prosperous countries, and the quality of life deteriorates; and yet I believe that what is being discovered about the infinitely large and the infinitely small is sufficient to absolve this end of the century and millenium. What a very few are acquiring in knowledge of the physical world will perhaps cause this period not to be judged as a pure return to barbarism.

# Beetles

It is said that the famous British biologist, J. B. Haldane, at a time when he was a convinced Marxist (and that was before the Lysenko scandal shook some of his certainties, asked by a churchman what his concept of God was, answered: 'He is inordinately fond of beetles.' I imagine that Haldane with the generic term 'beetles'* meant to refer to the coleoptera, and in this case we can only agree with him; for reasons that we do not know too well, this 'model', even within the multiform class of insects, numbers by itself at least three hundred and fifty thousand officially catalogued species, and new species are continually being discovered. Since many environments and many geographic areas have not yet been explored by the specialists, it is calculated that at present there exist one and a half million species of coleoptera. Now, we mammals, with our pride as the crown of creation, do not number more than five thousand species; at the very most a few dozen new ones might be discovered, while many existing species are rapidly becoming extinct.

And yet, the invention of coleoptera does not seem all that innovative: it consists 'only' in having changed the purpose of the anterior pair of wings. They are no longer wings but elytra: they are thickened and robust and act solely as protection for the posterior wings, which are membranous and delicate. Anyone who remembers the meticulous ritual with

* English in original.

which a cockchafer or a ladybird prepares for flight and has compared it to the lightning-like and oriented take-off of a fly, will have noticed that for the greater part of coleoptera flight in itself is not a way to escape aggression but rather a transportation system to which the insect has recourse only for long journeys: a bit like one of us who, to take an aeroplane, subjects himself to the business of buying a ticket, going through the check-in, and enduring the long wait at the airport. The cockchafer slightly opens the elytra, manoeuvres his wings, finally stretches them, lifts the elytra obliquely and begins his flight, neither agile nor swift. From this it seems one must conclude that a high price must be paid for a good cuirass.

But the coleoptera's armour is an admirable structure: to be admired, unfortunately, only in the glass cases of natural history museums. It is a masterpiece of natural engineering and reminds one of the all-iron armours of medieval warriors. It has no gaps: although not welded, head, neck, thorax and abdomen form a squat, practically invulnerable block, the tenuous antennae can be retracted into grooves and the legs' articulations are protected by flanges that recall the shinguards in the *Iliad*. The resemblance between a beetle that advances pushing aside the grass, slow and powerful, and a tank is so striking that it immediately calls to mind a metaphor in both senses: the insect is a small Panzer, the Panzer is an enormous insect. And the back of the beetle is heraldic: convex or flat, opaque or shiny, it is a noble escutcheon, even if its aspect has no symbolic relation to the 'trade' of its bearer, that is, its manner of escaping aggressors, reproducing and nourishing itself.

Here the Eternal's fondness for beetles has truly unleashed all his imaginative powers. There is no organic material, living, dead, or decomposed, that hasn't an enthusiast among the coleoptera. Many of them are omniverous, others feed at the expense of a single animal or vegetable species. There are those who eat snails exclusively and have turned themselves into a tool suited to this purpose: they are living syringes, their abdomen is voluminous, but head and chest have an elongated and penetrating shape. They plant themselves in the victim's soft body, inject it with digestive juices, wait for the tissues to disintegrate, and then suck them up.

The very beautiful cetonias or rosechafers (dear to the poet Gozzano: 'desperate cetonias overturned', one of the most beautiful verses ever composed in our language), feed only on roses, and the no less sacred scarabs only on bovine excrement: the male makes a small ball of it, clasps it between his hind tarsi as if between two pivots and takes off in reverse gear, pushing and rolling it until he finds a terrain suitable for burying it; at that point the female makes her entrance and deposits on it a single egg. The larva will feed on the matter (by now no longer ignoble) to which the farsighted couple has devoted so much effort, and after the moulting a new scarab will emerge from the tomb: indeed, according to some ancient observers, the same scarab as before, risen from death like the phoenix.

Other beetles can be found in slow or stagnant waters. They are splendid swimmers: some, inexplicably (who knows why?), swim in narrow circles or complicated spirals, others point in a straight line at an invisible prey. None of them, however, has lost the faculty of flying, for often necessity forces them to abandon a pond that has dried up to find another body of water, perhaps even far away. Once, travelling at night along a highway lit by the moon, I heard the windows and the roof of my car bombarded as if by hail: it was a swarm of diving beetles, shiny, brown, and edged with orange, as big as half a nut, who had mistaken the asphalt on the road for a river, and vainly tried to land on it. These beetles, for hydrodynamic reasons, have achieved a compactness and simplicity of shape which I believe to be unique in the animal kingdom: looked at from the back, they are perfect ellipses from which protrude only the legs transformed into oars.

In eluding dangers and aggressions also these insects 'think of everything'. Some exotic species, as large as a fava bean, are endowed with incredible muscular strength. If enclosed in a hand they force their way out between the fingers; if swallowed by a toad (by mistake, but toads will swallow any small object they see moving on a horizontal line), they do not follow the strategy of Jonah gulped down by the whale, nor that of Pinocchio and Geppetto in the shark's entrails, but simply, with the providential assistance of their front legs built to act as earth-movers, dig their way out through the body of the aggressor.

Other singular escapes are those of the click beetles, the elegant native beetles with an elongated body. If picked up or in any way disturbed, they retract legs and antenna and pretend to be dead; but after a minute or two a sudden click is heard, and the insect jumps into the air. For this short leap, taken to disconcert aggressors, it does not use its legs: it has elaborated a curious system of tension and snap. When in the position of feigning death, thorax and abdomen are not aligned but form a small angle: they straighten out with a snap when a kind of ratchet is released, and the click beetle is gone.

The cold light of fireflies (they too are coleoptera) is not aimed at defence, but serves to facilitate mating. And this too is an invention unique among animals who do not live in the water; but there are super-fireflies of a different species whose females imitate the steady light of the females of fireflies properly so-called, thus attracting their males and devouring them as soon as they alight beside them.

All these modes of behaviour evoke a complex range of impressions: amazement, curiosity, admiration, horror, and laughter, but it seems to me that over them all predominates the sensation of extraneousness or alienation. These small flying fortresses, these portentous little machines, whose instincts were programmed one hundred million years ago, have nothing at all to do with us, they represent a totally different solution to the survival problem. To some extent, or even only symbolically, we humans recognise ourselves in the social structures of ants and bees; in the industriousness of the spider, in the dance of butterflies: but nothing really ties us to the beetle, not even parental concerns, because among coleoptera it is very rare for a mother (and much less a father) to see its offspring before dying. They are the different ones, the aliens, the monsters. Kafka's atrocious hallucination is not chosen by chance – the story in which the travelling salesman Gregor 'awakening one morning from agitated dreams' finds himself changed into an enormous beetle, so inhuman that no one in his family can bear his presence.

So then, these different ones have shown how marvellous capacities of adjustment to all climates, have colonised all ecological niches and eat everything: some even perforate lead and tinfoil. They have elaborated an armour with extraordinary resistance to impact, compression, chemical agents and radiations. Some of them have dug shelters in the ground that are a metre deep. In the case of a nuclear catastrophe they would be the best candidates to be our successors (not the tumble bugs, who eat excrement, and these because of the lack of raw materials).

On top of everything else, their technology is ingenious but rudimentary and instinctive; after the planet becomes theirs, many millions of years will have to pass before a beetle particularly loved by God, at the end of its calculations will find written on a sheet of paper in letters of fire that energy is equal to the mass multiplied by the square of the velocity of light. The new kings of the world will live tranquilly for a long time, confining themselves to devouring each other and being parasites among each other on a cottage industry scale.

# A Bottle of Sunshine

It is not at all an idle matter trying to define what a human being is. If one limits oneself to the creatures existing in the world today, there are no ambiguities, but doubts arise and grow more and more gigantic as the discoveries of 'fossil men' accumulate; since when, at which genetic or cultural step, do they deserve the label *Homo*? Since when did our ancestors walk erect? Since when did they speak (but here, unfortunately, material proof is lacking, and will always be lacking)? Since when have they learned to make a fire? Since when have they instituted 'marriages, tribunals and altars'? As we see, the choice is broad and broadly arbitrary, so that I would dare to propose a further probability: man is a builder of receptacles; a species that does not build any is not human by definition. In short, it seems to me that to fabricate a receptacle is a clue to two qualities which, for good or evil, are exquisitely human.

The first is the ability to think about tomorrow. There certainly are animals 'not incautious of the future': ants, bees, squirrels, certain birds, and some of them in fact build receptacles: bees in particular, with admirable skill and economy of material, but their small hexagonal cell is only one, and their art, although at least one hundred million years old, has remained what it was, while ours, in a few millenia, has given origin to a myriad of objects. The second specifically human quality is the capacity to foresee the behaviour of matter: if we keep to the subject of receptacles, we know how to foresee what container and content 'will do', and how they will react to each other, at the instant of their contact and in time.

A boundless jungle of subjects has sprung from these two exigencies, each endowed with its own particular development; and, consequently, an assortment of receptacles (casks, pitchers, vials, bags, suitcases, baskets, sacks, buckets, ink stands, jars, goatskins, cylinders, boxes, bowls, crates, lead capsules for radioactive elements, cages, snuff boxes, trash cans, flasks for gunpowder, cans for tomato paste, mail boxes, velvet-lined jewel cases, scabbards for swords, pyxes for hosts, needle cases, air tubes, carry-this and carry-that, gasometers as large as cathedrals, cribs, urns, and biers) so jagged as to make one want to set up a classification, as one has always tried to do with animals, plants, and rocks.

There are receptacles, like vases and amphorae and bottles which have rapidly attained a perfect shape, and in substance have never changed. Given the problem (to contain a liquid without giving it extraneous odours or flavours; to stand upright on a support; to permit decanting without lateral losses), the solution was only one, and such it has remained. Now, instead, think of the heap of new problems which have accompanied the take-off of industrial civilisation: on the one hand, the appearance of substances with new, more precious, more aggressive properties; and on the other, and as a complement, more resistant, lighter or more economical building materials.

The kitchen itself, the most ancient of workshops and also the most conservative, has not withstood the impact of technological innovation. The copper utensils described by the novelist Nievo, the pride of the kitchen at Fratta, have almost disappeared, driven away by aluminium, which is less expensive, and by stainless steel, which lasts longer and does not dent: we find them displayed by antiquarians and junk dealers, but no one wants them any longer, not even as an ornament, and even less as a class symbol. In their place, even in the humblest kitchen today, one finds at least a hundred receptacles which can be catalogued under no less than twenty different species.

If we confine ourselves to those which the chemists call 'processing containers' (that is, those in which foods are cooked or fried and not simply preserved), for a first rough taxonomy the relation between the base area and height seems essential: pans when one wishes volatile products to disperse; pots or casseroles when one does not want the water to 'consume' too much; all the way to the hermetic pressure cookers, in which nothing, not even the aromas are lost. As for the 'service receptacles', the fable of the fox and the stork is still topical; Aesop was a man of genius.

The shape of these household objects is mostly rational, dictated by long experience; but a more attentive examination occasionally reveals stylised elements that are not rational, or are so no longer. In its usual shape, that is, of a thin, overturned, half cone, the spout of pots has no use at all; it idealises a channelling of the flow which in fact never occurs, neither with water nor with viscous liquids (and even less so with granular solids like peas).

A friend of mine, gifted with versatile talents, was the manager years ago of a factory in which, among other things, coffee pots were produced. He diligently studied the problem of the coffee's flow lines and derived from it an elaborate, crooked profile for the beak, very different from the traditional one. He made a prototype and verified that with it the coffee poured better, faster and with greater precision; he did not hesitate to change the moulds and go into production, but the result was disastrous. The consumer refused the new shape: the beak must be a beak, as the name says, and as it was in the Mycenean jars.

A receptacle is characterised not only by its shape but also by the material of which its walls are made. Naturally it must be impermeable to the liquid or gas one plans to store in it, but that is not enough. It must, for example, keep in the wine but let light through, and here the glass of bottles fulfills the task; or also stop heat from entering or exiting, hence the felt put round canteens or, more elegantly (but much more fragilely) the silvered, air-free space between the double walls proposed by Professor Dewar. He had designed it to store liquid helium, but today it serves excellently also for picnics. Or it must keep in the solids and let the liquids flow out, and as a result we have the innumerable progeny which run from the semi-permeable membranes of the inversely osmotic desalinators to the porous candles which are used to sterilise water, paper or canvas filters, strainers, mosquito nets, fishing nets, all the way to the barbed wire of battlefields and prison camps.

On the subject of selective walls, the very windows of our houses contain a small but refined arsenal of walls. Normal glass allows the passage of images but is a barrier to air and outside temperature; blinds, on the contrary, let in air but not light; shutters, neither air nor light; curtains, light and in part air but not images; frosted glass, neither images nor air; the window-grilles on the ground air, light images, even cats and stretched out hands, but not entire human bodies.

It is stimulating to think that our energy future, that is, our future *tout court*, depends exclusively on the solution of a receptacle problem. The machine for milking energy from nothing (from the water's hydrogen) already exists, not only on paper, and has proven tremendously efficient in hydrogen bombs. Still missing, and that alone, is the bottle whose walls resist the frightening temperatures the machine needs to function as the sun functions. To the gnomes who in the United States, the Soviet Union, but also at Frascati, are meditating on this bottle which will certainly turn out to be bodiless (it will be a magnetic field), it is in our best interests that we wish them good work and felicitous but not too audacious ideas. We do not know, nor do we know if they know, what might happen if their bottle were to break.

This seems to be the seal of our century. In our role as

builders of receptacles we hold in our hand the key to maximum benefit and maximum harm: two contiguous doors, two locks, but only one key.

# The Moon and Us *

More complex, more precise and more costly than a modern army, the great machine at Cape Kennedy moves ponderously towards the decisive moment. Within eight days, in an exactly predetermined instant and place, two men will set foot on lunar ground, marking a singular date in humanity's calendar, and translating into reality what in every century had been considered not only impossible but the paradigm, the customary synonym, for the impossible.

It will be necessary (or better, it would be necessary: common language is conservative, we still say 'he eats like four millstones' and 'at full stretch', when no one is any longer able to visualise the ancient allusion enclosed in these metaphors); it will be necessary to give up 'like living on the moon' understood as the symbol of vain fantasies, as a non-place; and yet it is amusing to remember how only twenty years ago, one spoke of the 'other side of the moon', as a typical example of inaccessible reality, by its essence unobservable. To discuss it was pure futility: like discussing the sex of the angels, or the Talmudic bird mentioned by Isaac Deutscher which flies around the world and spits on it every seventy years.

So we are about to take a great step: whether or not it is too long for our legs for the moment escapes us. Do we know what we are doing? It is permissible from many signs to doubt

* Article published just before the first landing on the moon by Aldrin and Armstrong, 21 July, 1969.

it. Certainly we know, and tell each other the literal, I was about to say the sporting, significance of the exploit: it is the most daring and at the same time the most meticulous ever attempted by man; it is the longest voyage, it is the most alien environment. But why we do it we do not know: the reasons cited are too many, too closely intertwined and at the same time mutually exclusive. At the basis of them all an archetype can be glimpsed; beneath the intricacies of the calculations lurks the obscure obedience to an impulse born with life and necessary to it, the same which impels the seeds of poplars to wrap themselves in fuzz, to fly far away on the wind, and frogs after their last metamorphosis to migrate obstinately from pond to pond at the risk of their lives. It is the impulse to disseminate, to disperse over a territory as vast as possible; because, notoriously, 'flower beds' make us ferocious and the propinquity of our fellows unleashes also in us men, as in all animals, the atavistic mechanism of aggression, defence and flight.

Despite the proud new science of 'futurity', we know even less where this step will take us. The great technological break-throughs of the last two centuries (the new metallurgies, the steam engine, electrical energy, and the internal combustion engine) have brought about profound sociological changes but have not shaken humanity at its foundations; on the contrary, at least for the big innovations of the last thirty years (nuclear energy, solid state physics, insecticides, fungicides and detergents) they have led to consequences which have a much greater scope and very different nature from what anyone dared expect. Among them at least three seriously threaten the vital balance of the planet's ecology and are forcing us to make hasty re-evaluations.

Despite these doubts, and despite the disastrous problems which besiege mankind, two men will tread the surface of the moon. We the multitude, we the public are by now habituated, like spoiled children: the rapid succession of spatial portents is extinguishing in us the faculty of wonder, though it is unique in man and indispensable in making us feel alive. Few among us will know how to relive, in tomorrow's flight, the exploit of Astolph * or the theological astonishment of Dante when he felt his body penetrate the diaphanous lunar matter, 'lucid, shining, thick, solid and clean'. It is a pity, but this time of ours is not a time for poetry: we no longer know how to create it, we do not know how to distil it from the fabulous events that unfold above our heads.

Is it perhaps too soon, do we only have to wait, will the poet of space come later? There is nothing to assure us of it. Aviation, the penultimate great leap, is already sixty years old, and has given us no other poet than St Exupéry and a step lower Lindbergh and Hilary: all three have drawn inspiration from precariousness, from adventure and the unforeseen. The literature of the sea died with the ships under sail; the poetry of railroads never was born, nor does it seem thinkable. The flight of Collins, Armstrong and Aldrin is too sure, too pro-grammed, not 'wild' enough for a poet to find nourishment in it. Of course, it is asking for too much, but we do feel cheated. More or less consciously we would like the new navigators to be endowed with this virtue too, besides the many others which make them outstanding: we would like them to know how to be able to transmit, communicate, sing what they will see and experience. It is unlikely that this will happen, tomor-row or later. From the black primeval vessel that has neither height nor depth, beginning nor end, from the region of Tohu and Bohu, until now no words of poetry have reached us, except perhaps a few naïve sentences from poor Gagarin: nothing but the nasal sounds, inhumanly calm and cold, of the radio messages exchanged with Earth, in conformity with a rigid programme. They do not seem the voices of man: they are incomprehensible as space, motion and eternity.

---

* In Ariosto's poem, he flies to the moon to recover the crazed Orlando's good sense.

# Inventing an Animal

To invent from nothing an animal *that can exist* (I mean to say that can physiologically grow, nourish itself, resist the environment and predators, and reproduce itself) is an almost impossible feat. It is a project that by far exceeds our rational abilities and also that of our best computers: we still know too little about existing vital mechanisms to dare create others, even only on paper. In other words, evolution has always proven itself to be enormously more intelligent than the best evolutionists. Every year that passes confirms the fact that the mechanisms of life are not exceptions to the laws of chemistry and physics, but at the same time the furrow which separates us from the ultimate comprehension of vital phenomena grows ever wider. It is not that problems are not solved and questions not answered, but every solved problem generates dozens of new ones and the process gives no sign of ending.

Nevertheless, the experience of three thousand years of storytelling, painting and sculpture shows us that even inventing at whim an animal from nothing, an animal whose ability to exist we do not consider important but whose image somehow stimulates our sensibility, is not an easy task. All the animals invented by mythology in all countries and all epochs are pastiches, rhapsodies of features and limbs taken from known animals. The most famous and most composite was the chimera, a hybrid of goat, snake, and lion, so impossible that today its name is equivalent to 'a vain hope'; but it has also been adopted by biologists to indicate the monsters they create, or would like to create, in their laboratories thanks to transplants among different animals.

The centaurs are fascinating creatures, the repository of multiple and archaic symbols, but Lucretius had already realised their physical impossibility and tried to demonstrate it with a curious argument: at the age of three the horse is at the peak of its strength, while man is still an infant and 'will often seek in his dreams for the nipple' from which he has just been weaned; how could two natures live together which do not *'florescunt pariter'* (bloom apace) and in any case are not inflamed by the same love?

In more recent times and in a beautiful science fiction novel, P. J. Farmer has indicated the respiratory difficulties of classic centaurs and solved them by endowing the centaurs with a supplementary organ similar to a set of bellows which draw in air through an aperture similar to a throat. Others have dwelt on the problem of nourishment, pointing out that a small human mouth would have been insufficient to feed the animal's equine part.

In short, it would seem that the human imagination, even when not faced by problems of biological verisimilitude and stability, hesitates to venture down new paths and prefers to recombine already known building elements. If one re-examines Borges' very beautiful *Manual of Fantastic Zoology*, one has difficulty finding in it a single truly original animal: there is not even one that vaguely approaches the incredible innovative solutions one can see, for example, in certain parasites like the tick, the flea, or the tapeworm.

In a sixth-grade class not far from Turin they carried out an experiment, having the children describe an invented animal, and the results confirmed this limit to the imagination. Substantially mythological, that is composite, animals were described: conglomerates of diverse limbs like Pegasus and the Minotaur, or flights into the colossal and the supernumerary which bring to mind Job's Leviathan, Rabelais' human and bestial giants, Argus of the hundred eyes, Shiva with his eight arms, Cerberus with his three heads, and the six-legged dog of the ENNI (Italian National Hydrocarbon Authority) logo. But within these limits bold, amusing and alarming intuitions have surfaced.

The *Executioner* lives underground because he fears the other horrible animals described by the other children, and sleeps twenty-two hours out of twenty-four. He eats only human flesh and fruit trees, and he can run as fast as one hundred and fifty miles an hour. The female is extremely fertile: 'She delivers almost eight or nine times a month, and always delivers fifty or sixty little executioners,' but the delivery also takes place in a cave because of the above-mentioned security reasons.

The *Lymph Dinosaur* also lives in a cellar, inside a box filled with paper and straw. The author does not mention its dimensions, which cannot be very large, but the story of the encounter with the animal evokes a subtle shiver of anxiety: the girl has gone several times down into the cellar to fetch wine, and has heard strange noises but she said nothing at home – 'as usual'. So there she is alone in the dark, in the dirty cellar, a place of atavistic fears, the urban and modern version of Hades; and lo and behold! the beast comes out into the open and the girl screams 'because it was terribly ugly'. The conclusion reveals an unfeigned anguish: 'I never want to see that animal again.'

The enormous *Neck-giant* is composite, as in any case are the two preceding animals ('it has the head of a swordfish ... and it is as heavy as a bull-dozer dog'), but differs from them due to a surprising characteristic: 'The woodcutters use it to saw wood.' Although this is not said explicitly it must be the fruit of a technological contamination. In fact 'it has six sections of its neck' (visible in the simple but precise illustrations supplied by the author: actually they are six vertebrae) 'which every now and then break and so when he goes to the mechanic he spends a lot of money and is poor.'

Then there is an animal with an unpronounceable eighteen-syllable name which 'has the characteristic of eating with its tail, so that the head watches out for danger'. An even more daring search for rationality is evidenced by the author of *Leptorontibus*, who is described with an unusual respect for verisimilitude. He has three eyes, is six feet tall and 'is afraid of everybody'. He does not have bones, 'and keeps upright by means of a complicated nervous system'. In this very odd zoo he is perhaps the only 'economic' specimen, whose author has set out only to arouse wonder or horror; 'he has only one lung and breathes through a hole situated at the top of his stomach': but this is an unusual stomach, for the animal, 'as soon as he is through chewing, he gulps down the food which does not descend through the tube but falls directly into a kind of sack that is supposed to be the stomach.' The author has also given thought to the embarrassing problems of excretion: 'to throw out the things he does not need he utilises the holes under his feet (which altogether are ten).' Who has not at least once in his life envied the modesty and discretion of the *Leptorontibus*?

The *Mostrumgaricos*, on the other hand, is completely out of line. He devours bisons and elephants: he attacks them in flight, diving headfirst from the trees and 'digging his sharp teeth into the brains of his prey'; he also breathes under water; weighs four thousand tons; his female delivers sixty cubs a month; his bones are harder than steel, and 'even when he falls, even from a mountain five thousand metres high, he doesn't hurt himself'; he has twelve hearts and sixty ribs and could be feared as invincible and immortal. However, 'he is afraid of only one disease, gloomititus, which for him is fatal.' In this last detail an archetype survives: there is no evil that can't be remedied, there is no invulnerability without its Achilles' heel.

There is the description, in truth rather sketchy, of another animal, unnamed but very intelligent and robust. 'When after looking high and low he doesn't find anything he is quite capable of dismembering even a small, innocent animal.' 'He has a beautiful pelt and ladies buy his fur for themselves.' His death is full of a tragic and solemn dignity: 'He can live only a certain number of years and when he knows that on a certain day he must die he begins to eat voraciously so as not to forget all the meals he once had.'

*Cocó* is surreal, meek and modest (he has only three eyes and is only twenty centimetres tall). I envy the amusement its author must have had in describing him. 'He eats stones, branches, flowers and cats': he comes from China but 'lives at No 2 Via Archimede' and plays with the children of the neighbourhood; on the other hand, he often lives in all parts of the town because he changes streets every day.' 'Now he is forty years old and smokes a pipe every five minutes,' but for him too a dramatic death lies in store: in fact Cocó 'lives until he is a hundred and then dies running, which is a tradition among these strange animals,' and at this point I cannot resist the temptation of re-quoting Tennyson, translated and quoted by Borges, the great depicter of strange deaths. Tennyson speaks of the Kraken, another invented animal, a gigantic squid a mile and a half long:

> Below the thunders of the upper deep . . .
> His ancient, dreamless, uninvaded sleep
> the Kraken sleepeth . . .
> There hath he lain for ages and will lie
> Battening upon huge seaworms in his sleep,
> Until the latter fire shall heat the deep;
> Then once for man and angels to be seen,
> In roaring he shall rise and on the surface die.

> (Borges, *The Manual of Fantastic Zoology.*)

This review would be incomplete if one did not remember the *Cibercus*. Its description begins in pallid tones; he has the usual six legs albeit thin 'as a blade of grass', the usual square ears, the eyes, one triangular and red, the other square and black, but the shock follows immediately: 'He has a tail two metres long and is made of cream.' On this note the text takes flight, carrying it coherently to its extreme consequences. The *Cibercus* 'lives in a cold forest, otherwise if he stayed in the sun he would melt'; he is weak and when an arrow strikes him it pierces him like nothing, then there is a legend . . . a herd of these animals came out into the sun to attack men, but as they came out they all melted.' Conscious of his comic talent, the author informs us that the *Cibercus* eats mice and chocolate, and he closes with the fatal thrust of the bullfighter's sword: 'This animal runs very slow.'

# The Leap of the Flea

The majestic metal wire armature of a crinoline, which belonged to some lady of the Czarist court, is exhibited at the Kremlin Museum. From the waistband, or rather from the horrifying metal hoop that serves as a waistband, hang two small tubes made of china, with the shape and size of specimen vials used by chemists; one reads on the description that they were traps for fleas. A teaspoon of honey was put at the bottom of the vial; the fleas, in their peregrinations between one fold of cloth and another, were attracted by the smell of the honey, entered the vial, slipped down its smooth sides, fell to the bottom and were stuck.

This is a chapter in a novel which describes the interminable struggle between two forms of cunning: the conscious, short-term cunning of man who must defend himself from parasites, invent his strategems in the course of a few generations, and the evolutionary cunning of the parasite which required millions of years but attains results that astound us.

Among animals it is precisely the parasites whom we should admire most for the originality of the inventions inscribed in their anatomy, their physiology and their habits. We do not admire them because they are a nuisance or harmful, but once we have overcome this prejudice an area opens before us in which, and this is the truth, reality far surpasses the imagination. It is enough to think of intestinal worms: they feed themselves at our expense with a food so perfect that, unique in creation together perhaps with the angels, they have no anus; or think of the fleas on rabbits whose ovaries, thanks to a complicated play of hormonal messages, work in syncrony with the ovaries of the host: thus rabbit and guest give birth at the same time, so that at birth each small rabbit receives his portion of minuscule larvae and will leave the nest already provided with fleas which are his contemporaries.

These are necessary stratagems. It must be remembered that the trade of parasite ('he who eats alongside you') is not easy, neither in the animal nor the human world. A good parasite must exploit a host larger, stronger and faster (or, in the human version, richer and more powerful) than he, but it is indispensable that he should make him suffer as little as possible, or he risks being expelled: and he mustn't cause his death (in human terms: go bankrupt), because then he too would be ruined. Think of mosquitoes and vampire-bats, which though so different from each other, have invented anaesthesia and use it in order not to disturb too much the sleep of the host during their modest removal of blood. A human analogy for this kind of anaesthesia could be found in the flattery of a powerful dispenser of benefits, but the parallel between human and animal parasites cannot be taken much further: in our complex society the sponging table companion has definitely yielded the field to parasitic classes and incomes against which it is more difficult to defend oneself.

An essential difference between human and animal parasites is established once and for all. The old-style human parasite had to be intelligent, because he lacked the appropriate instincts: for him, parasitism was a choice, and all his tricks had to be invented. The animal parasite, as far as one knows, is all instinct, is totally programmed, and his brain is small or absent. There is an economic reason for this; the hunt for the host, who is enormous and fast, is so uncertain that the species has preferred to invest its inventiveness not in the brain but in the digestive apparatus, not in the sensory organs but in the prodigious reproductive apparatus: the tapeworm, which lacks brains, digestive tract, and a locomotive apparatus, produces in its adult life several millions of eggs. This enormous compensatory fertility tells us that the tapeworm's 'infant mortality' is extremely high and that a larva's probability of having a career is in the magnitude of one in a million.

Man's fleas, from which we started, are no longer fashionable and nobody regrets their loss, but precisely now we are witnessing a mysterious revival of the louse, and so we must be on guard. It will help to remember that the flea, besides being a vehicle for epidemics, was only a few decades ago part of European civilisation and folklore, patronised all social classes (as shown by the above-described crinoline) and was often described by literary men. Bernardin de Saint-Pierre, who had boundless faith in Providence, declared that fleas are dark and are attracted by white cloth, so that men can catch them: 'but for the instinct for whiteness of these small, light, black, and nocturnal animals it would be impossible for us to see them and catch them' Giuseppe Gioacchino Belli, in a sonnet of 1835, paints this strangely sensual miniature of the 'flea-catcher', for whom there is no delight equal to that of catching fleas:

> Everyone has his favourite delight.
> I have the fleas. So there, I love
> To crack them and hear those little pops.

In Balzac's *Droll Stories* the nuns of the merry monastery of Poissy explain to a naïve novice how one must go about telling whether the captured flea is male, female, or virgin, but finding a virgin flea is extremely rare 'because these beasts are unmannerly, they are all lascivious sluts, who give themselves to the first comer'.

In the popular mind the flea, as for that matter also the fly, is related to the devil. In *Faust*, in the inn at Auerbach, Mephistopheles is applauded by everyone when he starts to sing the song of the king who had a huge flea, loved it like a son (not a daughter: *Floh*, in German is masculine), and kept him as a son and had a silk and velvet suit cut for him.

In truth, the flea's appearance under the microscope is so unusual as to appear diabolic, and diabolic is its ability to escape capture with a leap so swift that it abruptly eludes the eye and seems to disappear. It is precisely to this leap that an amateur rich in patience and ingenuity, Miriam Rothschild, has devoted herself for decades. It should not surprise us that a naturalist is not subject to our revulsions and taboos: from these studies have emerged facts so unusual as to deserve being known also by the layman.

The leap of the flea is commensurate to need: the leap of fleas that infest the mole, and on all animals that live permanently in a burrow, is short or even non-existent, because the initial assault of the sluggish and sedentary host, does not present problems. On the other hand, when the host is mobile and swift, like the cat, deer or man, it is essential that the insect, as soon as moulted, succeed in the fundamental undertaking of its life, which is the jump that takes it from the ground to its destination. Leaps thirty centimetres high have been measured on the human flea, which is to say at least one hundred times the flea's own length.

Now, the power required by such a leap cannot be supplied by a muscle, and even less by the muscle of an insect: at a low temperature the insects are practically inert, but the flea must jump 'without a warm-up' because its moulting takes place in environments that are not always heated, such as the floors of certain human habitations, and as soon as the flea emerges from the larval state it needs blood.

The problem thus stated, the elegant solution elaborated by evolution through the trials and errors of millions of years is the following. The powerful musculature which was assigned to the flea's flying ancestors, has been reconverted and connected to a system of elastic accumulation of mechanical energy: in substance, a mechanism of tension, release and snap similar to that of the crossbow of old or the spring-activated gun used by skin-divers today.

The elastically deformable organ, analogous to the gun's

spring and the crossbow's arch, is constituted by a protein almost unique in the animal kingdom, similar to rubber but with properties that have a much higher degree of performance. In this way the energy required for the instantaneous and prodigious leap is accumulated during a slower preparatory phase: between one leap and the next, the flea must 'collect itself', accumulate energy again for his springs; but even for these pauses it needs only a tenth of a second. And this is the secret which allows the insect to leap even in cold environments, and leap so high and so far.

Mrs Rothschild and her collaborators have understood and reconstructed these subtle phenomena by fabricating certain ingenious instruments, for example, very fast camera activated by the flea's take-off. Some readers will ask what is the use of all this research: a religious spirit might answer that the harmony of creation is also mirrored in the flea; a lay mind prefers to say that the question is not relevant and that a world in which only useful things are studied would be sadder, poorer, and perhaps even more violent than the world which fate has allotted us. In substance, the second answer is not very different from the first.

# Frogs on the Moon

The 'visit to the countryside' lasted as long as the school vacations, that is, almost three months. The preparations began early, usually in March on St Joseph's day: my father and mother roamed the still snow-covered valleys looking for a place to rent, preferably in some place serviced by the railroad and not too far from Turin. This was because they did not have a car (almost nobody had one) and because my father's vacation, although he hated the mugginess of summer, was no more than three days around the mid-August holiday. So just in order to sleep in the cool air and with his family, he subjected himself to the punishment of the daily train trip to Torrepellice or Meana or all the way to Bardonecchia. Out of solidarity, we went every evening to wait for him at the station; he left the next day at dawn, also on Saturday, to be in the office at eight o'clock.

Towards the middle of June my mother started packing. Apart from the bags and grips, the bulk of it was represented by three huge wicker baskets, which when full must have weighed at least two hundred pounds each: the porters would come, hoist them miraculously on to their backs, and carry them down the stairs, sweating and cursing. They contained everything: linen, pots, toys, books, provisions, light and heavy clothes, shoes, medicines, tools, as if we were leaving for Atlantis. In general the choice of the place was made in association with other families of friends or relatives; this way one was less lonely, and in short took along a piece of the city.

The three months went by slow, serene, and boring, studded by the sadistic abomination of vacation homework. They brought with them an ever new contact with nature: modest grasses and flowers whose names it was pleasant to learn, birds with various songs, insects and spiders. Once in the basin of the wash trough nothing less than a leach, graceful in its undulating glide through the water as in a dance. Another time a bat in the bedroom, or a weasel glimpsed at sunset, or a mole-cricket, neither mole nor cricket, an obese, repugnant and menacing little monster. In the garden-courtyard bustled orderly tribes of ants, whose cunning and obtuseness it was fascinating to study. Our school books set them up as an example: 'go watch the ants, you lazy-bones'; they never went on vacation. Sure, but at what price!

The most interesting place was the torrent where my mother took us every morning to be in the sun and splash about in the clear water, while she knitted in the shade of a willow tree. One could wade across it without danger from bank to bank, and it sheltered animals never seen before. On the bed slithered black insects which looked like large ants: each of them dragged along a cylindrical case made of pebbles or vegetal fragments in which it sheathed its abdomen, and from which only its head and tiny legs protruded. If I disturbed them, they pulled back with a jerk into their perambulating house.

Splendid dragonflies hovered in mid-air, with their deep blue, metallic reflections: also their buzz was metallic and mechanical. They were small war machines: they would suddenly plunge like arrows on an invisible prey. On the strips of dry sand ran green, very agile beetles and gaped the conical traps of the antlions. We watched their ambushes with a secret sense of complicity and therefore of guilt; to the point that my sister every so often gave in to compassion, and with a twig turned aside a little ant which was on its way to a sudden and cruel death.

Along the left bank pollywogs swarmed in the hundreds. Why only on the left? After much thinking we observed that along there ran a path frequented by the fishermen on Sundays, the trout had noticed, and gave it a wide berth, next to the right bank. The pollywogs in turn had settled on the left to keep away from the trout. They inspired conflicting feelings, laughter and tenderness like puppies, newborn babies, and creatures whose head is too large in relation to its body; and indignation, because now and then they devoured each other.

They were chimeras, impossible animals, all head and tail, and yet they navigated swiftly and surely, propelling themselves with an elegant waving of the tail. To my mother's disapproval I took a dozen home and put them in a basin whose bottom I had covered with sand taken from the torrent's bed. They seemed to be comfortable there, in fact in a few days they began to moult. Now this was really an unprecedented spectacle, full of mystery like a birth or a death, enough to make the vacation homework fade and the interminable days and nights fly by.

The pollywog's tail thickened into a small knot at its root. The knot grew; in two or three days two small, palmate legs sprouted from it, but the little animal did not use them: it let them hang inert, and continued to wag its tail. After a few more days a pustule formed on one side of its head; it grew, then burst like an abscess, and out of it came a little front leg, already nicely shaped, minuscule, transparent, almost a little glass hand that immediately began to swim. Shortly after the same thing happened on the other side, and at the same time the tail began to shorten.

It was obvious at first sight that this was a dramatic period. It was a brusque and brutal puberty: the little animal became restless, as if it were sensing within itself the travail of one who changes his nature and is upset by it, in the mind and entrails; perhaps it no longer knew what it was. It swam about frenetically and lost, with an ever shorter tail and four little feet still too weak for their purpose. It swam around and around, looking for something, perhaps air for its new lungs, perhaps a ramp from which to depart towards the world. I realised that the walls of the basin were too steep for the pollywogs to climb, as they obviously wanted to, and I put two or three small inclined wooden boards in the water.

The idea was correct and some pollywogs took advantage of it: but was it still right to call them pollywogs? No longer; they were no longer larvae, they were brown frogs, as large as a fava bean, but frogs, people like us, with two hands and two legs, who swam 'the breast stroke' with effort but perfect style. And they no longer ate each other, and by now we had a different feeling about them, maternal and paternal: in some way they were our children, even if in the moulting stage we had given them more trouble than help. I would put one of them on the palm of my hand: it had a muzzle, a face, it looked at me blinking its eyes, then it suddenly snapped its mouth wide open. Was it gasping for air, or did it want to say something? At other times it took off decisively along one finger as if on a springboard, and immediately made a crazy leap into the void.

Raising pollywogs was not all that easy. Only a few appreciated our life-saving boards and came up on dry land; the others who by now lacked the gills which had sustained their aquatic infancy, we would find drowned in the morning, worn out by too much swimming, just as would have happened to a human swimmer trapped between the gates of a lock. And the others too, the more intelligent, those who had understood the use of the ramps, did not live long.

A fully understandable instinct, the same that has propelled us to the moon, induces pollywogs to leave the expanse of water where they moulted; it doesn't matter where to, any place at all except that. In nature it is not improbable that near a puddle, or the bend of a torrent, there should be others, or in damp meadows or swamps; so some escape with their lives, migrate and colonise new environments, but at any rate even under the most favourable conditions a good part of them is destined to die. It is because of this that the mother frogs exhaust themselves in giving birth to interminable strings of eggs: they 'know' that the infant mortality will be frightfully high, and they provide, as did our great-grandparents in the countryside. We scattered our surviving pollywogs throughout the garden-courtyard in search of water that wasn't there. We pursued them in vain, amid the grass and stones; one, the most self-confident, who was thrashing about in little clumsy leaps trying to cross the granite pavement, was sighted by a robin who swallowed it in one gulp. At the same instant the white kitten, our playmate, who, stockstill, had watched the goings on, took a portentous leap and seized the bird, distracted by its lucky catch: she only half-killed it, as cats do, and carried it off into a corner to play with its agony.

# Love's Erector Set

One can fall in love at any age, in every case with emotions that are intense but dispersed over a vast spectrum that runs from the Edenic idyll to pervasive passion, from happiness to despair, from achieved peace to devastating vice, and from a communion of interests (also in business: why not?) to competitive polemic. When I was eleven years old, in the course of an interminable summer vacation, I fell in love with a certain nine-year-old named Lydia, polite, homely, sickly, and not all that bright. I gave her stamps for her collection, which in fact I had encouraged her to start, I shuddered with horror listening to her often repeated story about her tonsil operation, and I helped her with her summer vacation homework. Above all I was enchanted by her rapport with animals, which appeared magical to me, almost a divine gift: there was a German Shepherd who growled at everyone, perforated every rubber ball in sight with his canines and savaged the bicycle tyres of all the bike riders who rode past, but he let Lydia caress him, closing his eyes and wagging his tail, and in the morning whimpered in front of her door, impatient for her to appear; even the hens and chicks in the yard rushed to her at her call and pecked the feed out of the palm of her hand. I was reminded of Circe in the *Odyssey* which we had just read in school.

It would have been a sublime and serene love if I had not realised that the girl, affectionate with me, and grateful for my chivalrous services, nevertheless preferred another: Carlo, my best friend during those months, who was stronger than I. There was no point in deceiving oneself: that was the factor which determined Lydia's preference, and it was a massive, quantitative factor that could not be eliminated by propitiatory rituals. On the other hand, Carlo seemed completely indifferent to Lydia's timid advances: he preferred to play soccer, wrestle with the village kids, and pretend he was driving an old motorless truck that was rusting away in the middle of the meadow.

The foundation of my friendship with Carlo was the Erector set: we had nothing else in common, but this work-game tied us together for many hours of the day. I only had box No 4, and Carlo, whose family was richer, had box No 5, plus many supplementary pieces: altogether, almost the fabulous No 6. Both jealous of our property, we had stipulated precise agreements for the exchange, loan and common use of the pieces: putting together the two sets, our assortment was quite respectable. Playing with the Erector we were complementary; Carlo had good manual ability, I was better at project designing. When we worked separately, his products were simple, solid, and pedestrian; mine were fanciful and complicated, but not very stable because I neglected to tighten the bolts so as not to waste time; for this my father the engineer never stopped reproaching me. When we worked together, our virtues complemented each other.

In this situation, my double love for Lydia and the Erector set led to an obvious result: to seduce Lydia by means of the Erector. I knew better than to tell Carlo about my second ulterior motive, and confined myself to describing my project to him in its social aspect: for Lydia's nameday we would together build something never dreamed of, unique, never suggested even by the Erector set's unreliable illustrated booklets; and I thought to myself that Lydia would not be deceived, she would understand that Carlo, that Carlo of hers, was only the material executor, the bolt tightener, but that the inventor, the creator, was I, her devout admirer, and that the machine we were going to unveil in her presence was a personal and secret homage from me, a declaration in code.

What machine should we build? We discussed it: Carlo was far from intuiting the message I intended to entrust to the *opus*, and moreover, he had a small, spring-activated motor; he had clear, earth-bound ideas: we must make something that moved by itself, a car, an excavator, or a crane. I did not want one of the usual toys, indeed I did not want a toy: I wanted a gift, an offering. Symbolic, of course, to be recovered after the ceremony; I was in love, true enough, but I was certainly not about to make Lydia the actual gift of even a single perforated strip; and in any case, one does not make girls a gift of Erector pieces. I thought about it at length, then I proposed to Carlo that we build a clock. In today's memory I would not know how to justify this choice: perhaps I confusedly thought that a clock beats like a heart, or that it is faithful and constant, or perhaps I connected it up with the recurrence of the nameday.

Carlo looked at me perplexed: up to then we had been satisfied with simpler models, my project designer's audacity aroused in him at once distrust and respect; but a clock is driven by a spring, and therefore the little motor, his pride and my envy, would have found worthy employment. 'So let's do the clock,' he said in a challenging tone; and I in the same tone answered that there was no need for his motor: there was a time when clocks worked with weights, and ours would work like that. It would work even better, I explained, because a deformed spring loses force as it relaxes, whereas a descending weight exerts a constant force.

We set to work, I with enthusiasm, Carlo in a bad mood: perhaps he sensed the subordinate role I had preserved for him in my mind. The clock which grew under our hands was very ugly and did not look like a clock at all. In the beginning I meant to give it the shape of a grandfather clock, but I soon saw that our supply of pieces did not allow for the building of a tall, slim structure: the available girders were too weak. And yet it had to be tall because the weight needed space for its descent. I skirted the difficulty by fixing the shapeless device to the wall: the pendulum swung in the void, and the weight had one and a half metres of play. The escapement, that is, the device which transmits the pendulum's rhythm to the cylinder on which is wound the string of the weight and which regulates and brakes its descent, cost me a great deal of trouble: I think that I built it with two little bolts, one mine and one Carlo's.

The third of August, Saint Lydia arrived. I hoisted the weight and started the pendulum: the device started up with a scrap iron-like tick tock. I must point out here that I had not set out to build a clock that would mark time: the fact that the weight descended at a constant speed already seemed a victory to me, because we did not have gears that could transform the uniform motion of the cylinder into a cycle lasting exactly one hour. Our clock did have a cardboard face and a hand (only one), but it marked an arbitrary time: once around in twenty or twenty-one minutes, and shortly thereafter it stopped, because the pendulum was at the end of its run.

With unconscious cruelty Lydia asked me: 'What's it for?' She did not devote more than half a minute to our masterpiece: she was more interested in the cake and the real presents. I felt my mouth fill with the bitter taste of betrayal when I realised that the favourite present, the one Lydia showed proudly to her friends, was a small cellophane envelope: it had been given to her publicly, shamelessly, by Carlo, and contained a series of Nicaraguan stamps.

# The Invisible World

My father, who frequented as an expert the stalls on Via Chernaia where second-hand books were sold, brought home for me one day a small, elegantly bound volume, printed in London in 1846, whose title, at once modest and pretentious, was *Thoughts on Animalcules, or A Glimpse of the Invisible World Revealed by the Microscope.* By G. A. Mantell, Esq., LL.D., F.R.S. The title was followed by a high-sounding dedication: 'To the most Noble Marchioness of Northampton', which went on for twelve lines, some of them in Gothic characters.

I was fifteen years old, and was immediately transfixed: above all by the illustrations, because I did not know a word of English. But I bought a dictionary and was happily surprised to see that, contrary to Latin, this help was sufficient to understand anything, or almost: that is, I perfectly understand the text proper, in which the appearances and habits of the 'animalcules' were described with candid precision; I understand much less of the prolix preface in which were quoted Herschel and Shelley, Hobbes and Byron, Milton and Locke, and many other elect spirits who had in some way busied themselves with the invisible things suspended between earth and sky.

I had the impression that the author was somewhat confused between things one does not see because they are too small and those others one doesn't see because they are not there, such as gnomes, fairies, ghosts, and the souls of the dead; but the subject was so fascinating, so different from the teaching administered to me in high school, and so in tune with the curiosities I had at that time, that I buried myself in the small book for several weeks at the expense of my scholastic standing, though learning *en passant* a little English.

The book's epigraph was an electrifying dictum, hovering between the scientific and the visionary: 'In the leaves of every forest, in the flowers of every garden, in the waters of every brook, there are worlds pullulating with life, as innumerable as the glories of the firmament.' Could it be true? Literally, in the waters of every brook? Sudden and painful as a stomach cramp there grew in me the need for a microscope, and I told my father.

My father looked at me with a slightly alarmed eye. Not that he disapproved of my interest in natural science: he was an engineer, he had worked as a project designer in a large factory in Hungary; at that time he sold and installed electric motors, but in his youth he had been associated with the positivist circles in the Turin of those days: Lombroso, Herlitzka, Angelo Mosso, sceptical but easily deluded scientists who hypnotised each other, read Fontenelle, Flammarion and Annie Besant and went in for table-tapping.

My father had a love for science tinged with regret, and he would not have been averse to my following the path that he had been forced by the chances of life to abandon; nevertheless, it did not seem very natural to him that I, an adolescent, should desire a microscope instead of the many enjoyable and concrete things that the world offers. I believe he turned to someone for advice: the fact is that a few months later the microscope arrived at the house.

Seen in hindsight, that instrument wasn't worth much: it only enlarged two hundred times, was not very luminous, and had dizzying chromatic aberrations, but I immediately became attached to it more than to the bicycle which I had obtained after two years of petitions and cautious diplomacy. For that matter, the bicycle and the microscope were to a certain extent complementary: from the centre of town, how, without the bicycle, could I have reached the parks, forests, and brooks described by my book. In any case, before planning a sortie, I devoted myself to a microscopic inventory of everything that I could find on myself and around me.

The hairs I tore out had a completely unexpected appearance: they resembled the trunks of palm trees, and on looking closely one could make out on their surface those minuscule scales owing to which a hair seems smoother if run through two fingers from its root to its tip than the other way round: here was a first why to which the microscope gave an answer. On the other hand, the root of the hair, was rather repugnant; it looked like a softish tuber covered with warts.

The skin of the fingertip was difficult to observe, because it was almost impossible to keep the finger still in relation to the lens; but when one managed to do so for a few instants, one saw a bizarre landscape, which recalled the terraces of the Ligurian hills and ploughed fields: large, translucent, pinkish furrows, parallel but with sudden bends and bifurcations. A palm reader equipped with a microscope could have predicted one's future with more details than by examining the palm of your hand with the naked eye. It would have been very interesting, indeed in some way fundamental, to examine the blood and see the red globules described in the booklet, but I could not summon up the courage to prick myself, and my sister (who, for all that, proved singularly insensitive to my enthusiasms) curtly refused to prick me or let herself be pricked.

The flies, poor things, were a mine of observations: the wings, a delicate labyrinth of veins set in the transparent and iridescent membrane; the eyes, a crimson mosaic of miraculous regularity; the legs, an arsenal of talons, rigid hairs, and rubbery pads – slippers, foam-rubber soles and hobnail all in one. Another mine were flowers, beautiful or ugly, it made no difference whether beautiful or ugly; the petals didn't yield much (my magnification was not sufficient to reveal their structure) but each species deposited its pollen on the slide, and each pollen was very beautiful and specific: one could distinguish its separate granules, delicate and elegant architectures, small spheres, ovoids, polyhedrons, some smooth and shiny, others bristling with ridges or thorns, white, brown, or golden.

Just as specific were the shapes of the crystals one could obtain by letting the solution of various salts evaporate on the slide: common salt, copper sulphate, potassium bichromate, and others begged from the pharmacist; but here there was something new, one could see the crystals come to birth and grow 'under one's eyes'. At last something moved: the microscope was no longer limited to the immobility of vegetables and dead flies. It was curious that the first objects to move should be precisely the objects least alive, the crystals of the inorganic world, so perhaps this last term wasn't really so appropriate.

Also in the water of flower vases there was movement: and this indeed was not solemn and orderly like the growing of crystals. It was on the contrary turbulent and vertiginous enough to take your breath away: a pullulating which became more frenetic the longer the water had stagnated in the vase. Here they were, at last, the animalcules promised by my text: I could recognise them in the illustrations, delicate, meticulous, slightly idealised and patiently tinted with water colour (I'd become aware of this, having touched one when a small drop of water fell on it). There were big ones and tiny ones: some traversed the field of the microscope in a flash as if they were in a hurry to arrive at some distant place, others ambled lazily along as if they were grazing in a meadow, still others foolishly turned on themselves.

The most graceful were vorticellae: minuscule, transparent chalices which oscillated like flowers in the wind, tied to a twig by a filament which was long but so thin as to be barely visible. But the slightest tremor, grazing the barrel of the microscope with a fingernail, was enough and with a snap the filament contracted in a spiral and the opening of the chalice closed. After a few moments, as if it had overcome its fear the little animal relaxed, the filament stretched out again, and on looking closely, one saw the small vortex from which the vorticellae get their name: indistinct little crumbs rotated around the chalice and it seemed that some remained trapped within it. Every now and then, as if bored with sedentary life, a vorticella would lift the anchor, pull in the filament, and depart for adventure. It really was an animal like us, which moved, reacted, spurred by hunger, fear or boredom.

Or by love? The gentle poetic and perturbing suspicion came to me on the day when for the first time I had gone to Sangone by bicycle and brought home a sample of stagnant water and sand from the torrent, which then was clean. Here one could see monsters: enormous worms almost a millimetre long, which writhed as if tortured; other transparent beasties visible to the naked eye as tiny scarlet dots which under the microscope proved to bristle with antennae and hairy tufts, and moved in jerks like drowning fleas.

But the scene was invaded by the parameciums: tapered, agile, crooked like old slippers, they flashed by at such speed that in order to follow them the magnification had to be reduced; they navigated in the ocean of a drop of water, rotating on their axis, smashing into obstacles, and then immediately turning around and off again like crazed speed boats. They seemed to be hunting for light and air, solitary and bustling: but I saw two of them put on the brakes as if one had noticed the other, as if they had taken a liking to each other; I saw them get close, adhere tightly, and continue the voyage together at a slower pace. As if by this blind nuptials they had exchanged something and from it drew a mysterious, infinitesimal pleasure.

# A Long Duel

'There are those who like to gather the dust of Olympus on their chariot, and graze the goal with burning wheels'; thus, more or less, said Horace, and the small clan to which I belonged was shaken by a light and delicious electric charge. Ours was a monstrous *primo liceo* class made up of forty-one students, all males and almost all yokels, savagely impermeable to the knowledge that was being administered to us. Some rejected it or arrogantly derided it, others (the majority) let it run over them like irksome rain.

We were different. We were five or six, and *in pectore* proclaimed ourselves the élite of the class. We had elaborated a private morality, scandalously tendentious: studying was a necessary evil, to be accepted with the patience of the strong, since one did after all have to be promoted; but a precise hierarchy existed among the subjects. Excellent philosophy and the Natural Sciences; tolerable Greek, Latin, Mathematics and Physics, insofar as tools to understand the first two; indifferent Italian and History; pure afflictions Art History and Physical Education. Whoever did not accept this classification (which, unknown to us, had been generated chiefly by the talent and human warmth of the respective teachers) was automatically excluded from the clan.

There were other dogmas: about girls, and to girls, one must speak without sentimentalism, indeed in the crudest barracks language. The practices of swimming and fencing were admissible; accepted with suspicion was skiing, 'stuff for the rich'; soccer was disapproved of, because 'it hardens the knees'; tennis was excluded because effeminate, suitable for upper-class young ladies.

I, who in the summer played tennis at Bardonecchia, and even in mixed doubles, never confessed to it; but at any rate I was permanently at the fringes of the clan, accepted because I was good in Latin and passed on copies of the tests in class, envied because I possessed a microscope, but in odour of dissidence because despite my efforts, my vocabulary was not sufficiently vulgar. But the prince of athletics was track: whoever practised it was *ipso facto* an elect being, whoever ignored it was excluded. Two years before, at Los Angeles in 1932 Beccali had triumphed in the 1500 metres, and we all dreamed of emulating him, or at least excelling in some other speciality. Our small Olympics took place in the afternoon, in the stadium which stood where the Polytechnic Institute now stands.

It was a Pharaonic structure, one of the first of reinforced concrete erected in Turin: completed in 1915, it was already abandoned and disintegrating in 1934, an egregious example of the waste of public money. The ring of the track, 800 metres long, was by now bare soil strewn with holes, badly filled with gravel; weeds and scrubby little trees grew on the gigantic tiers. Officially entrance was forbidden, but we entered through the coffee bar, dragging along our bikes.

Some threw weights (a small block of cement), or a home-made javelin, some did the high jump or the long jump as best they could: but Guido and I kept strictly to the '*pulverem Olympicum*' sung by Horace. We had discovered that we were middle-distance runners, but Beccali's 1500 was too much for us; the dusty 800 metres of the track were plenty, and more than plenty for us. Those three verses reconciled us with things Latin; so those ancient Romans were not pure fossils: they knew the fever of competition, they were people like us. Pity they wrote in such difficult Latin.

Guido was a young barbarian with a sculptural body. He was intelligent and ambitious and envied my scholastic successes.

I, symmetrically, envied his muscles, his stature, his beauty, and his precocious sexual lusts. This intersecting competition had created a curious rough, exclusive, polemical friendship, never affectionate, not always loyal, which involved a continual contest, a confrontation to the bitter end, and in fact made us inseparable. We were fifteen or sixteen years old, and this competitive tension would have been almost normal if our weapons had been equal, but they were not. I enjoyed a certain initial advantage on the cultural plane, because at home I had many books and my engineer father brought me others by return post if I but hinted at a specific desire (except for Salgari, whom he detested and would not let me have), while my rival was the son of simple people. But Guido was neither stupid nor lazy, he borrowed all the books I talked to him about, read them voraciously, discussed them with me (we almost always had conflicting opinions) and then did not return them; so his cultural handicap was diminishing month by month.

On the contrary, his advantage on the physical plane was insuperable. Guido weighed a hefty sixty kilos of good muscle, and I only forty-five: any form of direct combat had to be excluded, but we had to and wanted to compete (perhaps I more than he), and before going down on to the track we invented various forms of indirect contests. For weeks on end we challenged each other to see who held his breath the longest; at first without particular conditions, then gradually refining our weapons. I invented the artifice of oxygenating my blood beforehand, by breathing long and deep before the contest; Guido discovered that one could gain a few seconds by competing lying on the ground instead of sitting up; I refined the technique of internal respiration, contracting and expanding my chest with my glottis closed. It worked, but Guido noticed the manoeuvre and immediately imitated it. We both resisted obstinately to the brink of passing out; we competed in turns, each holding the second hand in front of the increasingly bulging, glazed eyes of the other. There was no need for controls, it would never have occurred to us to cheat on the actual closing of the air passages, because each of us sought a test of personal will rather than the winning of a contest. I think that the results were not brilliant, we got up to one hundred seconds of apnoea, then, against our custom, we agreed to suspend the contest 'because otherwise we'll end up getting tuberculosis'.

The inventor of the slapping game was undoubtedly Guido. The rules, never written down or enunciated, had developed spontaneously: one must surprise the adversary's guard, on the street, at the desk, if possible even in school, and hit him full in the face, without warning, with as much strength as one could muster even in the middle of a peaceful conversation. It was permissible, indeed praiseworthy, to distract the adversary with chitchat, and even to hit him from behind, but only and always on the cheeks, never on the nose or eyes; it was forbidden to hit a second time, taking advantage of his dazed condition; admissible but almost impossible were parries; it was dishonourable to protest, complain, or be offended; obligatory to take revenge, but not right away, later on, or the following day, when fully relaxed, in the most abrupt and unforeseen manner. We had become extremely skilful at reading on the other's face the imperceptible contraction which was the prelude to the slap: 'Now you gape and roll your eyes, ready to wound,' I quoted from the *Inferno*, and Guido chivalrously praised me. Against all forecasts, I was the winner of the savage tournament, on points: my reflexes were faster than Guido's, perhaps because my arms were shorter, but my slaps which had reached the target, even if more numerous than his, were much less violent.

Guido got his own back easily in a contest which he himself had set up at a time when the striptease did not yet exist even in America; I was unable to overcome my modesty, I competed only once and stopped at the shoes. As I said, in this class we were all males; not all of us were blackguards, but the blackguards were the true leaders, not we 'intellectuals'. Guido challenged and defeated all of them. The test consisted in getting undressed in class, and this could take place only during the hours of natural sciences, because the professor was short-sighted and never came down among the benches. A few made it to a bare chest, four down to their shorts, but only Guido managed to strip from head to toe. The risk of being called to the blackboard was part of the game, and made it white hot: one could, in fact, occasionally see a student called for interrogation, struggling under the flap of his desk to get back into his trousers.

Guido, a strategist by instinct, had taken his precautions. With some excuse he had himself moved from the second to the last desk, had trained at getting his clothes back on in a hurry, had waited for the day after having been called for interrogation, and finally while the professor described the skeleton, indicating its parts with a pointer, he had not only stripped completely, but had climbed up first on to the seat and then on top of the desk, completely naked while we all held our breath, suspended between admiration and scandal. He stood there for a long instant.

Obedient to the collective myth, we had finally devoted ourselves to track; but it soon became evident that Guido would win hands down in all events but one, and this one was the 800 metres. And it was precisely in the 800 metres that he wanted to beat me, so that his athletic supremacy should be without flaw.

The first lap around the track would have laid out a beast. We wore tennis shoes and the gravel hurt our feet and reduced the spring of our stride. We had run together only once, massacring each other; neither of us wanted to be passed by even a few metres: we did not know that the more rational way of managing a competition consists in letting the adversary cut through the air for you, saving your breath for the final sprint. So, at the half-way point, we were both bushed; I slowed up, not out of generosity or calculation but due to total exhaustion; Guido, for honour's sake, went another dozen meters, then he too left the track.

From then on, each of us, terrified by the other's obstinacy, ran against the stopwatch; one scrambling up the track, the other following on his bike and announcing to him the partial times; but Guido was disloyal, instead of respecting my rabid concentration he told me dirty jokes to make me laugh. We went ahead with this for several weeks, filling our trachaea with Olympic dust, co-existing civilly in school, hating each other at the Stadium with the unconfessed hatred of athletes. At every encounter each of us summoned up all of his ferocity to nibble a few seconds away from the other's time.

At the end of the school year I stopped nibbling; Guido's superiority was proclaimed and consolidated; an abyss of at least five seconds separated us. Yet chance granted me a meagre victory: the bar in the stadium had gone out of business, and to enter the track one now had to scale the buttresses up to the top where some sort of passage had been left open. Now I realised that the gates which barred the entrance at ground level had sixteen-centimetre interstices: my skull just squeezed through, but at that time I was so skinny that if my skull got through the rest also got through easily.

Only I was capable of this exploit: well, wasn't that an event too? A gift of nature? like Guido's quadriceps and deltoid muscles? Stretching the terms a bit, as the Sophists used to do, it could be defined an athletic event whose modalities could be laid down by means of the proper regulations. Perhaps to the list of the undocile, the discontented begun by Horace, an *item* could be added, that of the gatecrasher. Guido did not seem very convinced.

I have lost track of Guido, and so I do not know which of us two has won the long distance race of life: but I have not forgotten that strange bond which perhaps was not friendship, and which united and separated us. In my memory his image has remained like this, fixed as in a snapshot: naked, standing on the absurd desk of the *liceo*, in symmetry with the obscene skeleton of which the professor was reeling off the inventory; so provocative, Dionysiac and obscene by juxtaposition, an ephemeral monument of terrestrial vigour and insolence.

# Grandfather's Store

My maternal grandfather had a store selling fabrics on the old Via Roma, before the pitiless disembowelment of the thirties. It was a long, tenebrous room with only one window, perpendicular to the street and below street level; a few doors down there was another, parallel cave, a café-bar that had been disguised to look like a grotto which had large stalactites of brownish cement in which were set tiny, multi-coloured mirrors; a profusion of small, vertical strips of mirror had been attached to the bottom of the counter. I do not know if by chance or deliberately the strips were not on an even plane but slightly angled in respect to each other: so, when passing before the threshold, one saw one's legs multiplied by the play of the mirrors, there seemed to be five or six instead of two, and this was so amusing that the children of that period – that is, we – asked to be taken to the Via Roma just for this.

My grandfather's name was not Ugotti but everybody called him Monsù Ugotti because he had taken over the business from a merchant who had this name. This merchant must have been a popular character because the name stuck for a long time also to my uncles and for several years after the war there still were people on Via Roma who even called me Monsù Ugotti.

My grandfather was a corpulent and solemn patriarch; he was witty but he never laughed; he spoke very little, in rare, exactly dosed sentences, dense with manifest and hidden meanings often ironic, always full of calm authority. I do not believe that he ever read a book in his entire life; the boundaries of his world were set by home and store, no more than 400 metres from each other, which he traversed on foot four times a day. He was a skilful businessman and at home just as skilled a cook, but he went into the kitchen only on great occasions, to prepare refined and indigestible viands; then he stayed in there for the whole day and sent away all the women, wife, daughters, and maids.

The personnel at the store was a curious collection of exemplary human eccentrics. Against a faded backdrop of hired clerks, who were often changed, stood out the perennial and amiable bulk of Tota Gina, the cashier. She made one flesh with the cash register and the high dais on which the register rested. From below, one saw her majestic bosom, which completely invaded the top of the desk and oozed over its edges like homemade pasta dough. She had teeth of gold and silver, and she made us presents of Leone candy drops. Monsù Ghiando spoke with pinched Rs and wore a wig. Monsù Gili wore flashy ties, ran after women and got drunk. Francesco (no Monsù for him, he was the handy man) came from Monferrato and they called him Iron Buster because he had once been attacked, had ripped out one of those long handles which served to raise the canopies, and had cracked his assailant's head. He could walk on his hands, he turned cartwheels, and after closing time he also performed somersaults over the sales counter.

Together with grandfather and the clerks, two of my uncles also sold fabrics. They would have probably liked to work at another trade, but grandfather's authority, never expressed in harsh words and even less with orders, was nevertheless undisputed and indisputable. Among themselves, the salesmen communicated in Piedmontese, though interspersing their speech with about twenty technical expressions which the customers (who were almost all women) could not decipher, and which represented a skeletal micro-jargon, an elementary

but essential code, whose terms were whispered rapidly and
with just the tips of barely moving lips.

It was composed first of all of numerals: reduced for simplicity's sake to a string of figures, naturally in cipher, which
were used by grandfather to transmit to the clerk what price
(reduced, or vice versa increased) to give to this or that
customer; in fact, the prices were not fixed, but varied in
relation to attractiveness, solvency, possible blood relationship,
and other indefinable factors. 'Missia' was a bothersome customer; 'tërdesun' (thirteen and one) was the most feared kind
of customer, who makes you pull down forty bolts from the
shelves, discusses price and quality for two hours and then
leaves without buying. In time, of course, the term was de-
ciphered precisely by a 'teres-un', (thirteen and one) who made
a big scene, and it was replaced by the equivalent 'savoia' (the
house of Savoy) which in turn did not last long. Other terms
simply meant 'yes', 'no', 'dig in', and 'let it go'.

Grandfather maintained cordial though diplomatically complex relationships with several competitors, some of whom
were also distant relatives. They exchanged friendly visits from
store to store, which were at the same time spy missions,
arranged Homeric Sunday meals, and called each other Signor
Thief and Signor Swindler. Also the relations with the clerks
were ambivalent: in the store they were absolute subjects; but
sometimes on Sundays, when the weather was fine, grandfather
invited them on social excursions to the Boringhieri beerhall
(on the present Piazza Adriano). Once, exceptionally, all the
way to Beinasco with the local train.

Utterly without shadows instead were his relations with the
other merchants who on Via Roma and its environs sold
shoes, underwear, jewellery, furniture, and wedding dresses.
Grandfather used to send the youngest and speediest clerk to
the Portanuova station to wait for the train's arrival from the
province: he was to pick out the engaged couples who came to
Turin to make their purchases and pilot them to the store. But
the young man's mission did not end with the purchase of the

cloth. He had to take the couple in tow to the other associated merchants of the consortium who, naturally, were organised to return the service.

At carnival time, grandfather invited all the grandchildren to watch the procession of allegorical floats from the store's balcony. At that time Via Roma was paved with delightful wooden tiles on which the iron hoofs of the draft horses did not slip, and along it ran the tracks of the electric trolley. Grandfather procured for us an adequate supply of confetti but forbade us to throw streamers, especially on damp days: in fact there circulated the legend of a little boy who had thrown a wet streamer over the trolley's cable and had been electrocuted on the spot.

At carnival time, as an exception, grandmother also came out on the store's balcony: she was a fragile little woman who wore on her face the regal air of the mother of many children, and had already, in life, the absorbed and timeless expression that emanates from the portraits of ancestors in their golden frames. She herself hailed from a vast family of twenty-one brothers, who had been scattered like the seeds of a dandelion in the wind: one was an anarchist and a refugee in France, one had died in the Great War, one was a celebrated rower and neuresthenic, and one (it was told, *sotto voce*, with a shudder) when he was still with his wet nurse had been devoured in his crib by a pig.

# Why Does One Write?

It often happens that a reader, usually a young person, will ask a writer, in all simplicity, why he has written a certain book, or why he has written in this way, or even, more generally, why does he write and why do writers write. To this last question, which contains all the others, there is no easy answer: not always is a writer aware of the reasons that induce him to write, not always is he impelled by only one reason, not always do the same reasons stand behind the beginning and end of the same work. It seems to me that at least nine motivations can be identified and I will try to describe them; but the reader, whether he is of the same trade or not, will have no difficulty in finding other reasons. Why, then, does one write?

(1) Because one feels the drive and need to do so. This, at a first approximation, is the most disinterested reason. The author who writes because something or someone dictates to him from within does not work with an end in view; he may obtain fame and glory from his work, but they'll be a bonus, an additional benefit, not consciously sought: in short, a by-product. Admittedly, the case outlined is extreme, theoretic, asymptotic; it is doubtful that there ever existed a writer – or in general an artist – so pure of heart. That's how the romantics saw themselves; not by chance we believe that we find such examples among the great men furthest from us in time, about whom we know little and who can therefore be idealised more

easily. For the same reason the most distant mountains appear to be of one colour, which often blends with the colour of the sky.

(2) To entertain others and oneself. Fortunately these two variants almost always coincide: it is rare that the person who writes to entertain his audience is not entertained by his writing, and it is rare that the person who enjoys writing does not transmit at least a portion of his enjoyment to his reader. In contrast to the preceding case, there exist pure entertainers, often not writers by profession, alien to ambitions, whether literary or no, lacking cumbersome convictions and dogmatic rigidities, light and limpid like children, lucid and wise like someone who has lived for a long time and not in vain. The first name that comes to mind is that of Lewis Carroll, the timid dean and mathematician who lived a blameless life and fascinated six generations with the adventures of his Alice, first in Wonderland and then behind the Looking-glass. The confirmation of his affable genius is found in the favour that his books enjoy after more than a century of life, not only with children, to whom he ideally dedicated them, but with logicians and psychoanalysts who never cease finding ever new meanings in his pages. It is likely that the uninterrupted success of his books is due precisely to the fact that they do not smuggle anything over on us, neither lessons in morality nor didactic efforts.

(3) To teach something to someone. To do this and do it well can be valuable for the reader but only if the terms are clearly stated. Except for rare exceptions, such as Virgil's *Georgics*, the didactic intention corrodes the narrative canvas from underneath, degrades and contaminates it: the reader who looks for a story must find a story and not a lesson he does not want. But, of course, there are exceptions and whoever has the blood of a poet knows how to find and express poetry when also talking about stars, atoms, cattle breeding and the

raising of bees. I would not like to shock any one by mentioning here *Science in the Kitchen and the Art of Eating Well* by Pellegrino Artusi, another man of pure heart who speaks without riddles: he does not pose as a literary man, passionately loves the art of the kitchen despised by hypocrites and dyspeptics, sets out to teach it, says as much, does so with the simplicity and clarity of someone who knows his subject deeply, and spontaneously produces a work of art.

(4) To improve the world. As can be seen, we are getting further and further away from the art that is an end in itself. It is appropriate to remark here that the motivations we are discussing have very little importance as regards the value of the work which they may originate; a book can be good, serious, durable and pleasing for reasons quite different from those for which it was written. Ignoble books can be written for the most noble reasons, and also, but more infrequently, noble books for ignoble reasons. However, I personally have a certain distrust for whoever 'knows' how to improve the world; not always, but often, he is someone so enamoured with his system as to become impervious to criticism. It is to be hoped that he does not possess too strong a will, otherwise he will be tempted to change the world with deeds and not merely words: this is what Hitler did after writing *Mein Kampf,* and I have often thought that many other Utopians, if they had sufficient energy, would have unleashed wars and slaughters.

(5) To make one's ideas known. He who writes for this reason only represents a reduced and therefore less dangerous version of the preceding case. In fact this category coincides with that of philosophers, be they geniuses, mediocre, presumptuous, lovers of mankind, dilettantes or madmen.

(6) To free oneself from anguish. Often writing represents the equivalent of a confession or Freud's couch. I have no objection

to the writer driven by conflicts: on the contrary I hope he will be able to free himself from them in this way, as happened to me many years ago. I ask him, however, to make an effort to filter his anguish, not to fling it as it is, rough and raw, into the face of the reader: otherwise he risks infecting others without getting rid of it himself.

(7) To become famous. I believe that only a madman would sit down to write just to become famous; but I also believe that no writer, not even the most unassuming, not even the least presumptuous, not even the angelic Carroll mentioned above, was ever untouched by this motivation. To be famous, to read about oneself in the newspapers, to be talked about – all this is sweet, there is no doubt; but few of the joys that life can offer cost so much effort and few efforts have such an uncertain result.

(8) To become rich. I do not understand why some people become indignant or are surprised when they discover that Collodi, Balzac, and Dostoevsky wrote to make money or pay gambling debts, or plug up leaks caused by bankrupt commercial enterprises. It seems right to me that writing like any other useful activity should be recompensed. But I believe that writing only for money is dangerous because it almost always leads to a facile manner, too obsequious to the taste of the largest audience and the fashion of the moment.

(9) Out of habit. I have left for last this motivation, which is the saddest. It is not good but it happens: it happens that the writer exhausts his propellant, his narrative charge, his desire to give life and shape to the images he has conceived; that he no longer conceives images; that he no longer desires anything, even glory or money; and that he writes all the same, out of inertia, out of habit, 'to keep his name in print'. He should be careful about what he is doing: he will not go far along that road, he will inevitably end up copying himself. Silence is more dignified, whether it be temporary or definitive.

# The Skull and the Orchid

Many years ago, shortly after the end of the war, I was subjected (indeed, I subjected myself: almost voluntarily) to a battery of psychological tests. Without much conviction, if not actually against my real feelings, I had applied to a big industrial company for a job; I needed work, but did not like big industries, I had ambivalent feelings and I hoped that my application would not be accepted. I received an invitation to take 'some tests', accompanied by the warning that their results would not have any influence on whether or not one was hired, but would prevent 'the round man from ending up in the square hole'. This bold image had astonished me and aroused my curiosity: I was younger than now and I liked new things. So let's try it, let's see how it works.

In the waiting-room I found myself in the company of about thirty other candidates, almost all male, almost all young, and almost all anxious. We underwent a cursory medical examination and an absentminded inquiry into our case history; all of this disagreeably reminded me in truth of a much more brutal ceremony which a few years earlier had marked my entry into the Lager: as if a stranger were looking inside you to see what you contained and what you are worth, as one does with a box or a bag.

The first test consisted in drawing a tree. After elementary school I had no longer drawn anything; however, a tree has specific attributes; I put them all in there and handed in the sheet. It couldn't have been a more tree-like tree.

The next test was more demanding: a young man with a rather unconvinced air handed me a booklet which contained 550 questions which were to be answered only yes or no. Some were stupid, others extraordinarily indiscreet, others yet seemed badly translated from a not-understood language. 'Do you sometimes think that your problems might be solved by suicide?' Perhaps I do, perhaps I don't, at any rate I'm not going to come and tell you. 'In the morning, do you have the sensation that the top of your head is soft?' No, honestly. 'Do you have or did you ever have difficulties in micturating?' The fellow next to me, who was from Taranto, nudged me with his elbow and asked: 'Colleague, what is this mentionating?' I explained and he was reassured. 'Do you believe that a revolution would improve the political situation?' You've got to be a wiseguy! I'm not a revolutionary, but even if I were . . .

The young man left with his booklets and a young, dark-haired girl made her entrance, obviously younger than the youngest among us. She told us to come one at a time into her office, which was nearby. When my turn came, she showed me four or five cards on which were printed enigmatic images, and asked me freely to express the sensations I experienced. One card depicted a small empty boat without oars, listing to one side and abandoned among bushes and trees. I said that an old maid of ours when we asked her 'How are you doing?' used to answer disconsolately 'like a boat in the woods', and the little girl seemed satisfied.

Another card showed some peasants who slept lying on the ground amidst sheaves of wheat, their hats pulled over their faces: they suggested to me thirst, hard work, earned and precarious rest. A third card bore the image of a young woman crouching at the foot of a bed in an unnatural and forced position, her head hidden between her shoulders and her back bent, as if she meant to make of that back an armour for herself against something or someone; on the floor there was an indistinct object that could be a pistol. I don't remember the subjects of the other cards; that work of interpretation suited me fine and made me feel at ease. The little girl said that she had noticed this, added no other comment and made me pass through into the adjoining room.

Here, seated behind a desk, was an elegant and extremely beautiful young woman. She smiled at me as if she had known me for a long time, had me sit down in front of her, offered me a cigarette and began to ask me technical questions, personal and intimate, on the order of those that confessors ask during confession. She was especially interested in my feelings for my mother and my father: on these she insisted annoyingly, but without ever relaxing her professional smile.

Now, at that time, I had already read my Freud and so did not feel completely unprepared. I got through it reasonably well, in fact, I even dared say to the beauty that it was a shame that we had so little time, otherwise we might have achieved a transference and I would have asked her out to dinner, but she cut me short, looking slightly annoyed. At this point the business was definitely beginning to amuse me: the anguish of feeling fathomed and weighed had disappeared.

There followed another small room and another lady examiner: she was older than her colleagues and also more bumptious. She didn't even look me in the face and fanned out ten Rorschach figures under my nose. They were large shapeless but symmetrical blotches, obtained by folding in two a white sheet of paper on drops of black or coloured ink: at first sight they can look like pairs of gnomes, or skeletons, or masks, or insects seen under the microscope, or nasty black birds; but at second sight they no longer mean anything. It seems that the way in which they are interpreted affords clues on the total personality of the individual. Now it happened that a few days before a friend had told me about these figures, and had also lent me the manual which accompanies them and explains with many curious details how their interpretation must be interpreted; that is, what is hidden inside the person who in the blotches sees a skull or, on the other hand, an orchid. It seemed to me proper to warn my examiner that the test would be flawed.

I told her so, and she became bloated with rage. How did I dare to commit such a transgression? It was unheard of: this was strictly their business, it belonged to them and laymen must not meddle with it. Theirs was a delicate profession and nobody must try to steal it. But above all: what was she supposed to write on my chart now? She certainly couldn't leave it blank. In short, I had put her in an impossible situation.

I took my leave with some indistinct apology, and filed away the whole business; when the letter hiring me arrived, I answered that I had already found another position, which was true.

Since then I have not been subjected to tests of this kind, and I am glad. I distrust them: it seems to me that they violate some fundamental rights of ours and that, besides all else, they are useless, because virgin candidates no longer exist. I like them, however, when they are approached as a game: they are then stripped of their pretentiousness, and indeed stimulate the imagination, give rise to new ideas, and can teach us something about ourselves.

# The Best Goods

The convention of Eastern European Judaism which took place in Turin in February, 1984, was the broadest on this theme ever held since the Second World War in Italy, and perhaps in all of Europe. It highlighted the enormous difference between this trunk of Judaism, which for centuries was the main one, and the many others, among which the Italian branch is included, and offered an excellent opportunity for rethinking for all those who attended it.

In the space of little more than one generation the Eastern Jews passed from a secluded and archaic way of life to lively participation in workers' struggles, national revindications, and debates on the rights and dignity of man (and of woman).

They were among the protagonists of the Russian revolution in 1905 and February 1917; during the 1920s, they printed in Warsaw alone no less than three daily newspapers and innumerable periodicals of all political tendencies; they were just in time, before the Nazi slaughter, to give life to an extremely original movie industry. Where did they find this portentous and sudden vitality? Where did they get this strong voice, which issued from such a small social body?

It is worth studying the reasons why these Jews 'weighed' so much, in countries where this weight of theirs was regarded with respect and simple curiosity, but most often with the old malevolence, envy, or actual savage hatred. I believe that, as always in the story of human affairs, there is not a single cause but rather an interlacing of causes; but among these, one seems to me to prevail.

There is one constant in Judaism, which operates in every time and place, and it is the importance which for centuries has been given to education. Beginning with the early Middle Ages a very peculiar system of education began to prevail among the Jews of Eastern Europe.

Education was considered life's supreme value: 'the best goods', as was proverbially said. It began at the age of four and continued throughout life, at least ideally and compatibly with the hardships of life itself; it was administered at the expense of the community, and almost no child went without it. The uneducated were pitied and despised, the learned were admired and *de facto* represented the only recognised aristocracy.

Certainly their educational methods were far from those which are prevalent today: one can get an idea of them from Chaim Potok's novels (*The Chosen* and those after it) which describe how such methods still survive, alongside more advanced pedagogic experiments, in the Chassidic communities transplanted in the United States.

Their foundation was strictly religious: immediately after learning the far from easy Hebrew alphabet, the child was set on the path of reading the Pentateuch and the literal translation from Hebrew into Yiddish of extensive passages; many other passages, even very long, must be learnt by heart. In subsequent years several commentaries on the Bible and the rules of life and prayer were studied. Our universities had their parallel in the rabbinical school, the Yeshivas, where study was extended to include the Talmud.

As we see, compared to modern tendencies this curriculum had many gaps: no history, geography, language of the place of residence; no, or almost no, exact and natural sciences; passing mention of the physician's art soaked in superstitious beliefs; little Western or lay philosophy; no literature, art, or music.

The teaching was burdensome and obsessive, and in the Yeshivas above all it took up the entire day, but it was not dogmatic. The teacher sketched a certain interpretation of a Talmudic passage, or pointed out some contradiction or other, or proposed a controversial topic: from this flowed a free, perfervid, sophistical discussion, occasionally witty, always obstinate: sometimes the central theme was forgotten, and a student ventured on imaginative divigations in which formal elegance or the audacity of the argumentation prevailed over relevance and rigour.

Wherever there was a synagogue, most likely an old wooden shack, there was also a library, naturally constituted only of religious books, but frequented by the young, adults and old people. Every community, even small, was therefore a 'hot-bed' of culture, set in a boundless territory where the non-Jewish population was almost totally illiterate, and the Jewish one, generally very poor, certainly was not composed of intellectuals with professions but of craftsmen, shopkeepers, merchants, and peasants. Then enforced multilinguism contributed to this educational pressure. Until the Hitlerian storm and along the vast arc of the once Czarist 'residential' zone, that is, from Poland and Lithuania to Moldavia and the Ukraine, the unifying spoken language in the archipelago of Jewish communities was Yiddish, with a few variations in lexicon and pronunciation: the 'mamaloshen', as it was affectionately called, that is, 'mama's language'; but quite soon, as mentioned, the children were taught the 'sacred languages', Hebrew and Aramaic, and furthermore the inevitable relations with the surrounding population obliged the Jews from childhood to learn the language.

In any case, Yiddish itself, a fascinating language for linguists (and not only for them), is intrinsically a multi-language: on the background of a medieval dialect of the Rhineland, which already contained borrowings from Latin and French, have been inserted many Hebrew and Aramaic terms, which often, nonchalantly, are declined or conjugated in the German manner (for example, from the Hebrew *ganav*, thief, comes a past participle *geganvet*, stolen), and a good number of Russian, Polish, Czech, etc., terms.

It is the language of a wandering people, driven by history from country to country, and it bears marks of each of its stations. And its evolution is not finished: the Yiddish of the Eastern Jews who in the last century emigrated to the United States is not extinct, indeed, it is being enriched with English terms, thus moving into a further evolution; symmetrically, the most expressive and least replaceable Yiddish terms enter 'from below' first into the various sectional jargons, then into the common language.

'Mama's language' is essentially spoken (although ennobled by a rich though belated literature), and this renders it eminently flexible and permeable; its extreme hybridism makes it an instrument for mental gymnastics both for the person who speaks it and for the person who tries to understand it and reconstruct its origins.

I believe that these cultural factors had a preeminent role in the brief but intense flowering of Askenazi Judaism; and, more generally, in the conservation, otherwise inexplicable, of the Jewish people throughout millenia of trials, emigrations and metamorphoses.

Certainly there have been and are other cements: religion, collective memory, common history, tradition, persecution itself, and the isolation imposed from outside. A counter-proof of this is the fact that, when all these factors become attenuated or disappear, the Judaic identity in turn becomes attenuated, and the communities tend to dissolve, as happened in Weimar Germany and is happening in Italy today.

It may be that this is the price to be paid for an authentic parity of rights and equality; if it were so, it would be a high price, and not only for the Jews. The slaughter and the dispersion of Eastern Europe's Judaism have been an irreparable loss for all of humanity. It is not dead, but survives badly: gagged and unrecognised in the Soviet Union, hybridised in the two Americas, submerged or drowned in Israel by different traditions and profound sociological and historical transformations.

Today one fears, and rightly so, the extinction of certain animal species, such as pandas and tigers. The extinction of a culture, portentously fertile and creative, as that to which the convention was dedicated, is a disaster of much greater scope. A funereal echo should be sounded in all minds by the verses of Itzhak Katzenelson, the Warsaw poet massacred at Auschwitz with all his family and all his people, verses which were saved against all odds:

The sun, rising over the land of Lithuania and Poland,
will no longer meet one Jew,
Not one old man reciting a psalm by a gay little window.

# The Scribe

Two years ago, I bought myself a word processor, that is, a writing tool that returns automatically at the end of a line and makes it possible to insert, cancel, instantaneously change words or entire sentences; in brief makes it possible to achieve in one leap a finished document, clean, without insertions or corrections. Certainly I'm not the first writer who has decided to take the plunge. Only a year ago I would have been considered reckless or a snob; today no longer, so fast does electronic time run.

I hasten to add two clarifications. In the first place, whoever wants to, or must, write can very well continue with his ballpoint or typewriter: my gadget* is a luxury, it is amusing, even exciting, but superfluous. Secondly, to reassure the uncertain and laymen, I myself was, in fact still am, as I'm writing here on the screen, a layman. My ideas as to what takes place behind the screen are vague. At first contact, this ignorance of mine humiliated me profoundly; a young man rushed in to reassure me and he has guided me. To start with, he said to me: 'You belong to the austere generation of humanists who still insist on wanting to understand the world around them. This demand has become absurd: leave everything to habit, and your discomfort will disappear. Consider: do you know or do you think you know how the telephone and television work? and yet you use them every day. And

* English in original.

with the exception of a few learned men how many know how their hearts and kidneys work?'

Despite this admonition, the first collision with the apparatus was filled with anguish, the anguish of the unknown which for many years I had no longer felt. The computer was delivered to me accompanied by a profusion of manuals; I tried to study them before touching the keys, and I felt lost. It seemed to me that although they were apparently written in Italian, they were in fact in an unknown language; indeed, a mocking and misleading language in which well-known words like 'open', 'close', and 'leave', are used in unusual ways. To be sure, there is a glossary that strives to define them, but proceeds in an opposite direction to that of common dictionaries: these define abstruse terms by having recourse to familiar terms; the glossary would give a new meaning to deceptively familiar terms by having recourse to abstruse terms, and the effect is devastating. How much better it would have been to invent a decisively new terminology for these new things! But once more my young friend intervened and pointed out to me that trying to learn how to use a computer with the help of manuals is as foolish as trying to learn how to swim by reading a treatise without going into the water; indeed, he specified, without even knowing what water is, having heard only vague talk about it.

So I set about working on two fronts: that is, verifying the instructions of the manuals on the equipment, and immediately the Legend of the Golem came to mind. It is told that centuries ago a magician-rabbi built a clay automaton with Herculean strength and blind obedience so that it would defend the Jews of Prague from the pogroms; but it remained inert, inanimate, until its maker slipped into its mouth a roll of parchment on which was written a verse from the Torah. At that, the clay golem became a prompt and wise servant: it roamed the streets and kept good guard, but turned to stone again when the parchment was removed. I asked myself whether the builder of my apparatus happened to know this strange story (they certainly are cultivated and even witty people): in fact the computer actually has a mouth, crooked, slightly open in a mechanical grimace. Until I introduce the programme floppy disk, the computer doesn't compute anything, it is a lifeless metallic box; but, when I turn on the switch a polite luminous signal appears on the small screen: this, in the language of my personal golem, means that he is avid to gulp down the floppy disk. When I have satisfied him, he hums softly, purring like a contented cat, comes alive and immediately displays his character: he is industrious, helpful, severe with my mistakes, obstinate, and capable of many miracles which I still don't know and which intrigue me.

Provided he's fed the proper programme, he can run a warehouse, or an archive, translate a function in his diagram, compile histograms, even play chess: all undertakings that for the moment do not interest me, indeed, make me melancholy and morose, like the pig who was offered pearls. He can also draw and this for me is a drawback, of the opposite sort: I hadn't drawn anything since elementary school and now, having available a servo-mechanism which fabricates for me, custom-made, the images that I cannot draw, and at a command even prints them right in front of my nose, amuses me to an indecent extent and distracts me from more proper uses. I must do violence to myself to 'leave' the drawing-programme and go back to writing.

I have noticed that writing in this way one tends to be prolix. The labour of the past, when stone was carved, led to the 'lapidary' style: here, the opposite takes place, the manual labour is almost nil, and if one doesn't control oneself one inclines to a wasteful expenditure of words; but there is a providential counter and one must keep one's eye on it.

If I now analyse my initial anxiety, I realise that it was in great part illogical: it contained an old fear of those who write, the fear that the unique, inestimable text worked at so hard, which will give you eternal fame, might be stolen or end up in a manhole. Here you write, the words appear neatly on the

screen, well aligned, but they are shadows: they are im-
material, deprived of the reassuring support of the paper.
The written word speaks out; the screen doesn't; when you're
satisfied with the text 'you put it on disk', where it becomes
invisible. Is it still there, absconding in some little corner of
the memory disk, or did you destroy it with some mistaken
move? Only after days of experience *in corpore vile* (that is,
on false texts, not created but copied) do you become convinced that the catastrophe of the lost text was foreseen by
the talented gnomes who designed the computer: the destruction of a text requires a manoeuvre which has been made
deliberately complicated, and during which the apparatus
itself warns you: 'Watch out, you're about to commit suicide.'

Twenty-five years ago I wrote a not very serious short story
in which after many de-ontological hesitations, a professional
poet decides to buy an electronic Versifier and successfully
delegates to it all his activity. My apparatus for the time being
does not do as much, but it lends itself in an excellent fashion
to the composing of verses, because it permits me to make
innumerable changes without the page looking dirty or dis-
orderly, and reduces to a minimum the manual effort of
writing: 'So one observes in me the counterpart.' A literary
friend of mine objects that in this way one loses the noble joy
of the philologist intent on reconstructing, through successive
erasures and corrections, the itinerary which leads to the
perfection of Leopardi's *Infinite*: he's right, but one can't have
everything.

As far as I'm concerned, since I've put bridle, bit and saddle
on my computer the tedium of being a Dinornis, the survivor
of an extinct species, has become attenuated in me: the gloom
of being 'a survivor of his own time' has almost disappeared.
The Greeks said about an uncultured man: 'He doesn't know
how to read or swim'; today one would have to add 'Nor how
to use a computer'. I still don't use it well, I'm not learned,
and I don't know if I ever will be, but I am no longer illiterate.

And besides, it is a pleasure to be able to add an item to one's list of memorable 'firsts': the first time you saw the sea; passed the border; kissed a woman; gave life to a golem.

# 'The Most Joyful Creatures in the World'

Recently, Ceronetti, Semioticist that he is, 'reread' the *Song of the Sylvan Cock*; by a curious coincidence it happened that almost simultaneously I reread, as the zoologist that I am not, 'In Praise of Birds' by Giacomo Leopardi. After decades of intensive and widely popularised ethology, the impression one derives from it is singular and vaguely alienating, similar to that which one might derive from contemplating Venus in the early morning (it is at the height of its splendour precisely during these serene dawns) after having read that its effulgency sung by innumerable poets is an effect of the reflection of solar light by an atmosphere like that of Dante's *Inferno*, unbreathable, scorching, super-pressurised, and, what's more, saturated with clouds of sulphuric acid. In either case, the poetic discourse which we perceive in the nature around us is not interrupted, but has changed intonation and content.

It is not that the desolate message of 'In Praise of Birds' has lost its value. If we limit ourselves to the sparrow family, which is familiar to us, those of our orchards, hills and gardens, birds are for us too 'the most joyful creatures in the world'. They seem joyful to us because fate has allotted them song and flight, and such they seemed to Leopardi also, because nature, which has endowed them with very acute senses, has also given them 'a very strong imaginativeness', though it is not 'profound, perfervid and tempestuous', but instead light and variable, like that of children, to whom birds are also close due to their continuous and apparently useless vivacity.

According to Leopardi, it is possible for them to be joyful because they are released from the awareness of life's vanity. Therefore, they do not know boredom, an affliction typical of the conscious man and all the more painful for him the further he moves away from nature. Moreover, they are protected from the extremes of cold and heat; if the environment becomes hostile to them they migrate until they find better living conditions. But, even though independent and free by antonomasia, they are still sensitive to the presence of man, and their voice is gentler where the customs of humanity are gentler.

This song of theirs, in which Leopardi sees the peculiarity of birds, is the sign of their happy condition: it is gratuitous, it is a song-laughter, 'a demonstration of gaiety', capable of transmitting this gaiety to the listener, 'bearing continuous witness, even though false, to the felicity of things'. Also the birds' restlessness, their 'bodies never remaining still', is a pure manifestation of joy, it takes place 'without any necessity whatsoever', and their flight is 'for pleasure'. In conclusion, Leopardi, or, more correctly, the fictitious ancient philosopher to whom 'In praise' is attributed, would like (but only 'for a short while') 'to be changed into a bird, so as to experience that contentment and the gaiety of their life'.

These are limpid, firm pages, valid for all times, whose strength comes from the constant but unexpressed comparison with the wretchedness of the human condition, with our essential lack of freedom symbolised by our being weighted to the ground. However, we may ask ourselves how Leopardi would have written them if instead of basing himself on Buffon, and limiting himself to birds whose song he listened to during the long evenings in his town, he had read for example the books of Konrad Lorenz and extended his attention to other species of birds. I believe that in the first place he would have abandoned every attempt to compare birds to men. To attribute to animals (with the exclusion perhaps of the dog and certain monkeys) feelings such as gaiety, boredom, and happiness is admissible only in poetry, otherwise it is arbitrary and highly misleading.

The same can be said about the interpretation of the birds' song: ethologists explain that the song, especially if solitary and melodious (and therefore most pleasing to us), has a well-defined meaning of territorial defence and admonition to possible rivals or invaders. Therefore, much less than to man's laughter, it is comparable to unfriendly human products, such as the fences and gates with which owners surround their property, or the insufferable electronic sirens meant to keep thieves from breaking into apartments.

As for the vivacity of birds (some birds: others, for example wading birds, are quite calm), this is an obligatory solution to a problem of survival: it is observed chiefly in birds who feed on seeds and insects and must therefore engage in frenetic activity in their search of food, which is scattered over vast areas, and often not very visible; on the other hand, the high body temperature and the effort of flight make it necessary for these birds to eat a great deal. As we can see, it is a vicious circle: labour to procure food, eat to repair the damages of labour; a closed circuit not unknown to a good part of mankind.

With these reductive observations I am not in the least trying to prove that admiration for birds is not justified. It is so fully, even if we accept the explanations which scientists (not without polemics among themselves) continue to supply us with: indeed, above all if we accept them, although they focus on different and more subtle virtues.

How, for instance, could one not admire the adaptability of starlings? Deeply gregarious, they have lived seemingly since always in cultivated countrysides, where sometimes they massively looted the vineyards and olive groves, but now during the last decades they have discovered the cities: it seems that they settled in London in 1914 and that a few years ago they arrived in Turin. Here they have chosen for their winter dormitories some large trees on Piazza Carlo Felice, Corso

Turati and elsewhere, whose branches, when they are bare in the winter, seem laden with strange, blackish fruits.

At dawn they leave in compact regiments 'for work', that is, for the fields beyond the industrial belt; and return home at sunset in gigantic swarms, of thousands of individuals, followed by scattered stragglers. Seen from a distance, these flights look like clouds of smoke: but then, of a sudden, they display themselves in astonishing evolutions, the cloud becomes a long ribbon, then a cone, then a sphere; at last it spreads out again and like an enormous arrow points unwaveringly at the nocturnal shelter. Who commands this army? And how does he transmit his commands?

Nocturnal predators are extraordinary hunting machines. Their appearance, unusual and slightly clumsy when they are at rest, has always aroused curiosity and sometimes aversion. Their flight is silent, their claws powerful, and they have large frontal eyes which confer upon them a vaguely human appearance; but even the largest and most sensitive eyes are blind in complete darkness. And yet, in rigorous experiments it has been observed that an owl is capable of seizing a mouse with the speed of lightning, even in total darkness, so long as the mouse makes even the slightest noise. Localisation of prey is accomplished through the sense of hearing, and probably the asymmetry of the bird's ears which has been long observed is also involved; but how the acoustic signals are elaborated is, for the time being, a mystery.

Even denser is the mystery surrounding the orientation of birds. It is known that not all migratory birds orientate themselves in the same way, and that many dispose of different strategies at the same time, and make use of one or the other depending on environmental conditions; certainly geographic points of reference on the ground and the position of the sun come into play; probably also the earth's magnetic field and the sense of smell.

But we are spellbound and struck by an almost religious awe when reading that some migrants who fly only on clear nights not only orientate their flights by the stars, but from the configuration of the sky draw with precision the point at which they are; or to which they were transported for purposes of an experiment; and that capable of so much are not only the birds who already followed the swarm during previous migrations but also the young individuals on their first flight. In short, everything takes place as if they were born already in possession of a celestial map and an internal clock independent of local time, stowed in a brain that weighs less than one gram.

No smaller is our astonishment at the behaviour of the cuckoo, which in the light of our human morality seems to be dictated by a perverse cunning. Instead of building a nest, the female deposits her egg in the nest of a smaller bird; the legitimate owners of the nest often (not always) do not notice the intrusion, hatch the alien egg together with their own, and the small cuckoo breaks the shell. Barely born, still featherless and blind, he already possesses a characteristic sensitivity and intolerance: he can't stand other eggs near him. He pushes and shoves until he has managed to make all the eggs of his putative brothers fall to the ground.

The two 'parents' continue to feed him feverishly for days and days, until the chick is much bigger than they are. One has the impression of reading a bad serial novel, and one doesn't know whether to be more surprised at the perfection of the cuckoo's instincts, or the lack of such instincts in his involuntary hosts: but in nature's games there must after all be a winner and loser.

Birds, like other animals, do not know how to do all the things we do, but perhaps know how to do other things that we do not know how to do, or not as well, or only with the help of instruments. If the experiment dreamed of by Leopardi could be realised, we would resume our human form with several more arrows for our bow in our quiver.

# The Mark of the Chemist

They say that Free Masons used to recognise each other by scratching each other's palms while shaking hands. I would propose that the chemists (or ex-chemists like myself) of my generation when they are introduced to each other should each show the palm of the right hand: towards the centre, where the tendon that flexes the middle finger crosses what palm readers call the life line, the majority of them have a small professional, highly specific scar whose origin I will explain. Today in chemistry laboratories even the most complex apparatuses can be set up in a few minutes by using cone-shaped, frosted, integrated glassware: it is a rapid and clean system, the joints hold well even under vacuum, the pieces are interchangeable, there is a vast assortment of them, and assembling is as simple as playing with Lego or an Erector set. But until around 1940 integrated cones were unknown or extremely expensive in Italy, and at any rate out of the reach of students.

Plugs of cork or rubber were used for retention; when (a frequent thing, in order, for example, to connect the flask to a cooler) you had to slip a tube of glass bent at a straight angle into a pierced plug, hold it and turn it while pushing, the glass often broke, and the sharp stump plunged into your hand. It would have been simple, indeed a matter of duty to warn adepts of this small, easily preventable danger: but it is known that in some obscure tribal recess of our nature survives an instinct that impels us to make sure that every initiation be painful, memorable and leave its mark. This here, in the palm of the working hand, was our mark: the mark of chemists still to some extent alchemists, still somehow members of a secret sect.

In any event and still on the subject of hermetic retention, the older professors spoke with curious nostalgia about the 'luti' used by the pioneers of chemistry at a time when the plugs did not exist: they were mixtures (*lutum* in Latin is mud) of clay and linseed oil, or of litharge and glycerine, or of asbestos and silicate, or still others, which were used to connect their crude apparatuses. The reddish window putty based on red lead which has not been used for a couple of decades is its distant offspring.

Entering the laboratory for the first time really had something of the initiatic ritual. There was the white smock for boys and girls: only heretics desirous of appearing as such wore grey or black. There was the spatula in the breast pocket, the insignia of the guild. There was the ceremony of the handing over of the glassware: fragile, sacred because fragile, and if you break you pay; for the first time in your career as a student, indeed in life, you answered for something that wasn't yours, that was solemnly entrusted to you (against a signed receipt).

A curious commerce was born from it. Often a glass carelessly exposed to the open flame gave off a sinister *tick* and cracked. If the crack was small you pretended that nothing had happened, hoping that when the glassware was returned the man in charge of supplies would not notice it; if it was large, the piece was put on auction: it could still be useful. It could be useful to the student who had spoiled a preparation, or who had scattered a precipitate to be weighed, or who at any rate, also for private reasons, needed to blow off steam; for a few lire he bought the damaged glass, and publicly, with the greatest violence and the worst possible racket flung it against the wall over the sink.

The enormous sink and its environs were the seat of a

perennial assembly. One went there to smoke, to chat, and also to court the girls: but laboratory work, especially analysis, is serious and absorbing, and even when courting it was difficult to shrug off the anxiety connected with it. There was a lively exchange of information, advice, and complaints.

It was strange: being forced to take an oral exam again certainly wasn't pleasant, but it was approached in a sporting spirit by the person involved and his colleagues; it was more an accident than a failure, it was a mishap to be described later with a certain amount of amusement, almost a boast, as when one twists an ankle skiing. To botch an analysis was worse: perhaps because unconsciously one realised that the judgement of men (in this case the professors) is arbitrary and debatable, while the judgement of things is always inexorable and just. This law is the same for all.

No one who 'lost' an element in qualitative analysis ever boasted about it; even less boasting was heard from someone who had 'invented' an element, that is, had found in the mysterious gram of powder which was assigned to us, something that was not there. The former might be distracted or short-sighted, the latter could only be a fool: it is one thing not to see what is there, it is another to see what is not there.

Under many aspects the two analyses, qualitative and quantitative, differed from everything we had seen or done until then. Not by chance were individual values overturned, as had happened with physical education in high school. The 'top students in the class', those of proverbial memory, triumphant at oral exams, expert at disentangling the intricacies of theoretical chemistry, expert at presenting clearly the ideas acquired in class, or passing off as understood things they hadn't understood, capable of appearing assured even when they were not, sometimes even endowed with superior intellect, when confronted by laboratory work did not always do well. Other virtues were required here: humility, patience, method, manual dexterity; and, also, why not, good eyesight, a keen sense of smell, nervous and muscular stamina, resilience when faced by failure.

Above all, quantitative analysis, in its variation called pon-deral, was an exhausting exercise. The pedagogue, professor or assistant gave every student a vial which contained, in solution, an unknown quantity of an element. We had to 'precipitate' it, that is, render it insoluble by means of a certain reagent and according to rigid modalities; collect *all of it* (often this work took hours) on a filter: wash it, desiccate it; calcinate it; let it cool and weigh it on the precision scales. The sequence left no room for initiative, involved unnerving stretches of dead time and maniacal attention; it was not an attractive task, it re-sembled too much what a machine could do (and in fact, machines do it today, much better and faster than men). I can confess it, now that many decades have passed: the top score that I obtained in 1940 in the exam of quantitative analysis was not merited, or rather was a reward for an ambiguous merit. I had thought of compiling the results obtained by my colleagues in the dosage of the element on which the practical exam hinged, and had noticed that, aside from small dis-parities, they were 'quantified': they were whole multiples of a certain value. There was nothing metaphysical about it and the meaning was clear: in order to save time and effort the professor, instead of weighing his little portion for each candi-date, more or less at random, must have used a burette, that is, a long vertical tube calipered and graded, assigning to each a whole number of cubic centimeters of solution.

I made sure of it one day by going, with some excuse, into the secret room where the practical quizzes were prepared: yes, the burette was there, for all to see, still full of a light blue solution. It was enough to perform the analysis even hastily and then round out the result in such a way that it cor-responded to the closest degree on my table. I communicated my illegal discovery only to two intimate friends, who received top scores like me.

I don't know whether tests in quantitative analysis are still ad-ministered in this way. If so, let this confession be noted by lazy professors and students. Unfortunately, the trick is worthless in the innumerable practical instances in which the chemist, by now graduated, is placed before the sad task of a quantitative determination of matter of vegetable, animal, or mineral (or even commercial) origin. As is known, nature does not take leaps, or at least not macroscopic leaps.

In the laboratory the girls were more at ease than the boys. At a time when, at least in Italy, feminism had as yet no weight, the girl students saw a reassuring continuity between housework and lab work: the latter was just a little more precise in its prescriptions, but the analogy was obvious, and the discomfort of the new experience was proportionately less. Among us it had become a pleasant custom for our colleagues at five to offer tea prepared in the lab glassware; sometimes even accompanied by minuscule experimental cookies, hurried and profanatory confected with starch and diastase and baked in the small oven for the desiccation of precipitates.

Despite the drawbacks mentioned above, I believe that every chemist preserves a pleasant, nostalgic memory of the university lab. Not only because in it there was nurtured an intense camaraderie linked to the common work, but also because one left it every evening and more acutely at the end of the course with the sensation of having 'learned how to do something'; which, life teaches, is different from having 'learned something'.

# Eclipse of the Prophet

Nowadays there is much talk about malaise, and round tables and conventions are devoted to the subject. Malaise does exist, there is no doubt: it is, however, a compendious term which covers different phenomena, and in a different degree for each country. It would be a black humour to speak of malaise for the places where people die of hunger, thirst, disease, and war: let us confine ourselves to the countries we know better, and in which 'one lives well'; to Europe in particular.

The European today does not fear European or civil wars; he is not hungry; if he falls ill, he does not die in the middle of the dust but finds more or less efficient succour; his children have a reasonable probability of reaching an adult age; he lives better than his fathers and his grandfathers; and yet he experiences malaise and to this malaise he gives various names. The biggest cause for malaise is, or should be, nuclear fear. Under this aspect, the situation is new in human history: it has never happened, not even distantly, that a single act of will, a single gesture, could lead to the instantaneous destruction of the human species and the probable disappearance within a few weeks of every form of life on Earth.

This fear is strange and shapeless: it is too vast to be accepted rationally. It does not weigh on us as one would expect: it has assumed the form of an obscure malaise, due precisely to the novelty of our condition for which we are not prepared. It exists, and has been theorised about in terms of a 'mathematical fear', which is mathematical hope with an inverted sign; that is, it is the product of the expected damage (or, respectively, advantage) multiplied by the probability that it will take place. This concept is abstract and it does not help us. Here the damage is maximum: is it infinite? No, because death, even if horrendous, even of everyone, puts an end to suffering: but it is still a boundless damage. But what may be its probability, which is the second factor, we do not know. Unknowingly, imperceptibly, each of us has estimated it to be minimal, close to zero, so that the product, our fear, remains within bearable limits and allows us to sleep, eat, make love, procreate children, take an interest in the soccer championships, watch TV, and go on holiday. We have been able to make this reductive evaluation (which can, of course, even be correct) exactly because this scenario is new: we lack the only instrument that helps us estimate the probability of a future event, that is, the count of how many times and under which circumstances it has taken place in the past.

This instrument is useful only when the event has occurred many times: grave international tensions are followed by wars, and wars, experience tells us, are followed by epidemics and famines. But here there is no experience: total, ubiquitous, definitive war is a new fact, confronted by which we are all *tabulae rasae*. New is the damage, new is the ignorance of its probability. Our only hope is founded on the reflection that the great statesmen must after all know that they too would end up in the furnace, together with their subtleties and their systems. This is not an entirely unfounded hope, and, besides, it is magnified by our tendency to push away fear.

More precisely: there exists a tendency, irrational but observed over the centuries, and well in evidence in situations of danger, to carry the probability of a terrible event close to its extreme values, zero and one, impossibility and certainty. We noticed this in the Lager, that ferocious sociological observatory. If I am permitted to quote myself, almost forty years ago, in *If This is a Man*, I wrote:

If we were logical, we would resign ourselves to the evidence that our fate is beyond human knowledge, that every conjecture is arbitrary and demonstrably devoid of foundation. But men are rarely logical when their own fate is at stake; on every occasion, they prefer the extreme positions. According to our character, some of us are immediately convinced that all is lost, that one cannot live here, that the end is near and sure; others are convinced that however hard the present life may be, salvation is probable and not far off, and if we have faith and strength, we will see our houses and our dear ones again. The two classes of pessimists and optimists are not so clearly defined, however, not because there are many agnostics, but because the majority, without memory or coherence, drift between the two extremes according to the moment and the mood of the person they happen to meet.

It seems to me that, with the exception of a few changes in the unit of measure, these observations are valid also for the world in which we Europeans live today, free from need but not from fear. Apparently the entire gamut of the possible is difficult for us; total credulity or incredulity are the preferred alternatives, and among these the second prevails. We are extremists: we ignore intermediate ways, we are desperate or (as today) carefree; but we live badly. And yet we should reject our innate tendency towards radicalism, because it is a source of evil. Both the zero and the one leads us to inaction: if the future damage is impossible or certain, the 'what to do?' ceases. Now, this is not how matters stand. The nuclear holocaust is possible, and more or less probable, depending on a great number of factors, including our single behaviours, individual and collective. It is not easy to say what we must do, but certainly in all our private and political choices we must never forget the fact that the future is *also* in our hands, it is plastic and not rigid. In particular it must not be forgotten by those who are closest to power: the politicians, the military, the scientists, the great technicians. If they will unleash the apocalypse, they too will be swept away by it, and uselessly: to everyone's damage and no one's advantage.

A good part of our malaise comes therefore, I believe, from the extreme unknowability of the future, which discourages every long-term project of ours. The human condition did not appear like this even twenty years ago. We were not so disarmed, or rather we were but did not notice it. We have always lived in terms of models, golden and distant idols, and we have demonstrated a singular versatility (and ability to forget) in dismissing old models and taking on new, different, or even diametrically opposed ones: so long as there was a model. Pliny already mentioned the improbable Hyperboreans, beyond the snowy and gelid Ripei mountains, who live long and happily in a country of eternal spring (although the night there lasts six months), and kill themselves only because they are sated with living. We've had Eden, Cathay, Eldorado: in Fascist times we chose as our model (here too not without reason) the great democracies; then, depending on the moment and our propensities, the Soviet Union, China, Cuba, Vietnam, Sweden. They were preferably distant countries, because a model by definition must be perfect; and since no real country is perfect, it is advisable to choose vaguely known remote models that can be safely idealised without fear of a conflict with reality. In any case, we manufactured a goal for ourselves: our compass pointed in a definite direction.

Parallel with the models, we followed men who were made like us of Adam's clay, but we idealised them, made them gigantic, worshipped them like gods: they could do and could know everything, they were always right, they had the license to contradict themselves, to wipe out their past. Now the delirium of delegating seems to have ended, both in the West and in the East: no longer are there the Happy Islands nor the charismatic leaders (perhaps the last ill-omened specimen is Khomeini and he won't last long). We are orphans, and live in the malaise of orphans. Many of us, almost all of us, had found it convenient, economic, to put our faith in a ready-made truth: it was a human but mistaken choice, and now we pay for its failure. Our future is not written, it is not certain: we have awakened from a long sleep, and we have seen that the human condition is incompatible with certainty. No prophet dares any longer to reveal our tomorrow to us, and this, the eclipse of prophets, is a bitter but necessary medicine. We must build our own tomorrow, blindly, gropingly; build it from its roots without giving in to the temptation to recompose the shards of old shattered idols and without constructing new ones.

# Stable/Unstable

I recently read with genuine pleasure that the firemen's provincial headquarters will soon distribute (in the schools, I imagine) ten thousand copies of a manual for the prevention of accidents, in particular fires in the home. With pleasure, wondering why nobody had thought of it before, and with a small pang of nostalgia for my previous trade, in which the fear of fire was the constant preoccupation of all working hours (and also many leisure hours), but in recompense forced us to be ready and vigilant at all times, and brought us back to the times when that fear was acquired in childhood and preserved all through life, because houses were then built of wood.

Anyone who has had the opportunity to handle wood for professional, craft, or amusement reasons knows that it is an extraordinary material, hardly equalled by the most modern plastics. It has two great secrets: it is porous and therefore light, and it has very different properties with the grain or against the grain; it is enough to think of the different effect produced by an axe blow from on top of a block of wood or across it. 'Ugly' wood does not exist, and there does not exist a tree whose wood has not found its specific application: the cedar for pencils, the linden tree for piano keys, balsa for the remote vessels which set sail from South America for the unknown West, but also for the chairs which movie actors break over each other's heads in the collective brawls.

For thousands of years wood has been a construction

material, the 'material' *par excellence*, so much so that in some languages *material* and *wood* were referred to by the same word. There is no doubt that our ancestors, ten thousand, one hundred thousand years ago, long before learning how to melt bronze, had learned how to work with wood. And yet, alongside their bones are flints, shells, bronze, silver and gold, but never wood (or only under absolutely exceptional conditions) and this should put us on the alert.

It should remind us that wood, like all organic substances, is stable only in appearance. Its mechanical virtues go hand in hand with an intrinsic chemical weakness. In our atmosphere rich in oxygen, wood is stable more or less like a billiard ball placed on a horizontal shelf edged by a border no thicker than a sheet of tissue paper. It c  remain there for a long time, but the tiniest push, or even a faint breath of air, will be enough to make it go past the barrier and drop to the ground. In short, wood is anxious to oxidise, that is, to destroy itself.

The path to destruction can be very slow, can take place silently, coldly, as in buried wood through the agency of air helped by the bacteria underground; or it can be instantaneous, dramatic, when the impulsion comes from a source of heat. Then there is fire: a rare event in our cities of concrete and glass, but frequent in the past period. Its memory is alive where one still builds with wood. Many years ago in Norway I slept in a very beautiful hotel built entirely of wood, in the middle of a boundless and silent forest. In every room in the corner there was a rolled up hauser, with one end free and the other attached to the floor: in case of fire it would have served to let oneself down to the ground through the window.

Because the enemy of wood is air, or rather, the air's oxygen, it is understandable that the danger to wood increases with the amount of air surrounding it: thin sheets of wood, sticks, dowels, shavings, sawdust. This last, especially, is a source of danger and I hope it is not neglected in the manual mentioned above: because it is widely used and because it is often piled up and forgotten as if it were any inert material. It is not always inert, particularly when it is dry.

In a factory where I worked for many years sawdust was generally used to clean the floors. We knew it as a substance which should not be trusted, so we did not keep it inside the department: once we bought ten barrels of it and stored them in the open under a shed; nobody thought to close them with a cover because the cleaning men often came to get some and because 'that's how it's always been done'. The barrels remained there for several months, until a foreman came to tell me that smoke was issuing from one of the barrels. I went to look: nine barrels were cold, the tenth was burning hot and from the top of the sawdust rose a streak of sinister smoke. We dug in with a shovel: at the centre of the barrel there was a nest of embers and the sawdust all around it had already begun to carbonise. If we had kept that barrel in one of the departments or the warehouse the entire factory would have gone up in flames.

Why one and not the other nine? We discussed this at length and then decided to take a closer look at the surviving barrels and we noticed that the sawdust was not at all homogeneous: perhaps it came from different sawmills, it certainly was composed of different woods. It probably also contained extraneous material. All this could explain why the barrels had behaved in different ways, but it wasn't much help in understanding why one of them had caught fire in that way. Then someone began to talk about auto-combustion and everybody felt reassured, because when one gives a name to something one doesn't know, one immediately has the impression that one knows it a little better.

At any rate I went to tell the story to the chief of firemen at that time, a solid and practical man. No, he had no clear ideas on auto-combustion, on the contrary he considered it a bogus name, a word to cover up ignorance, like the physicians' crypto-genetic fever; he had, however, seen several cases like ours, not all involving sawdust, some of which ended in catastrophe, all of them connected by one disquieting feature. In all of them, an apparently inert mass forgotten somewhere, in an attic, a cellar, or a dump, suddenly, under an almost always unknown stimulus, 'remembered' that it possessed energy, that it was out of balance with the environment, in short, that it was in the position of that billiard ball on the shelf.

The contours of this fragile stability which chemists call metastability are ample. Included in them, besides all that which is alive, are also almost all organic substances, both natural and synthetic; and still other substances, all those that we see change their condition of a sudden, unexpectedly: a serene sky, but secretly saturated with vapour, which in a flash becomes clouded; a quiet stretch of water which below zero freezes in a few instants if a pebble is thrown into it. But the temptation is great to stretch those contours even further, to the point of enclosing in them our social behaviours, our tensions, all of today's mankind, condemned and accustomed to living in the world in which everything seems stable and is not, in which awesome energies (I am not speaking only of the nuclear arsenals) sleep a light sleep.

# The Language of Chemists (I)

Although their trade is more recent than that of theologians, vintners or fishermen, chemists too, since their origins, have felt the need to equip themselves with a specialised language of their own. Nevertheless, unlike all other trade languages, that of chemists has had to adapt itself to rendering a service which I believe is unique in the panorama of the innumerable specialised jargons: it must be able to indicate with precision, and if possible describe, more than a million distinct objects, because that is the number (and it grows every year) of the chemical compounds found in nature or constructed by synthesis.

Now, chemistry was not born all of one piece like Minerva, but laboriously, through the patient but blind trials and errors of three generations of chemists, who spoke different languages and often communicated with each other only by letter; therefore the chemistry of the past century was gradually consolidated through a terrible confusion of tongues, whose vestiges still survive in the chemistry of today. Let us for the moment leave aside inorganic chemistry, whose problems are relatively simpler and deserve a separate discussion. In organic chemistry, that is, in the chemistry of carbon compounds, at least three different modes of expression flow together.

The most ancient is also the most lithe and picturesque. It consists in giving each newly discovered compound a fanciful name, which harks back to the natural product from which it was isolated for the first time: names like carotene, lignin, aspargine, abietic acid express fairly well the origin of the substances but say nothing about its constitution. Even more obscure for us neo-Latins is adrenalin, which was named like this because it was isolated from sub-renal capsules ('*ad renes*', that is, renal, close to the kidneys). Also benzine derives its name (in Italian and German: other languages have different names for it) from a natural product, but through a strange and tangled chemico-linguistic history. At the beginning there is benzoin, a scented resin which for at least two thousand years was imported from Thailand and Sumatra and which at one time was used not only for perfumes but also for therapy: I do not know on what grounds, perhaps only because of the dangerous reasoning according to which substances that have a pleasant smell are 'good for you'. The trade in this resin and many other spices was in the hands of Arab merchants and navigators. Since the penchant for advertising and with it the protection of commercial secrets are as old as trading itself, the Arabs sold the product under a pretty but deliberately misleading Arab name: they called it 'Luban Giaví' which means 'Java incense', although benzoin was not a real incense and did not come from Java at all.

In Italy and France the first syllable was mistaken for an article and has fallen off: what remained of the name, that is, Bengiaví, was pronounced and written in various ways until it became established as *benzoé*, *beaujoin*, *benjoin*, and finally *benzoino*. More centuries passed, until in 1833 a German chemist was the first to think of subjecting benzoin to dry distillation, that is, heat it at high temperature in the absence of water, in one of those retorts which to this day appear here and there as heraldic symbols of chemistry, even though chemists no longer use them. It was believed at that time, more or less consciously, that this treatment served to separate the volatile, noble, 'essential' part of a substance (not for nothing is gasoline still called 'essence' in French) from the inert residue which remained at the bottom of the retort: in short it was believed that a soul was being separated from a body. In fact in many languages, the word 'spirit' designates the soul, as well as alcohol and other liquids which evaporate easily.

Thus the German chemist obtained the 'soul', the 'essence' of benzoino and called it benzine: in actuality it was the product that we today called benzene, but with the analytical means of the time it was not easy to distinguish it from the fraction of petroleum which has approximately the same point of distillation and today is called gasoline: during the first decades of the past century the two names and the two products were substantially interchangeable, and at any rate even today benzene could be a good gasoline surrogate if it were not so toxic. Many partisan automobiles ran on benzene and even more exotic and dangerous fuels without obvious harm. It is only a curious coincidence that a man who in 1885 built the first efficient gasoline-fuelled motor was called Benz; unless his name (which is still part of the corporate name of Mercedes) contributed to Engineer Karl Benz's vocation as an inventor.

Also from dry distillation and the aim of isolating the essence, the spirit of wood, begins the history of methane's name. Through the dry distillation of wood, complex liquids are obtained, very different depending on which one sets out from, and in any case made up in large part of water. However, they often contain a small percentage of what is today called methyl alcohol.

Another chemist, French this time, in the last century purified this 'wood spirit', described its properties, and noticed that it closely resembled the old and well-known 'wine spirit'; its aroma and taste were even more agreeable than those of the latter, but consumed even in small quantities it resulted in permanent blindness, and thus it confirmed that a pleasant odour is a very bad guide. Probably with the help of some Hellinist colleague he badly translated 'wood spirit' as a '*methy hyle*' because in Greek *hyle* is wood and *methy* generically indicates intoxicating liquids (wine, fermented honey, mead, etc.). This '*methy*' also appears in the very ancient name of the amethyst: not because of its purplish colour but because it was believed that this gem had the property of combatting intoxication.

From '*methy hyle*' was derived 'methyl alcohol', and from this the name of methane, which is chemically close to it, on the basis of a first rudimentary agreement among the chemists of various countries, according to which the ending '-ane' was to be reserved for saturated hydrocarbons. Methane was followed by ethane which has the root of 'ether'; propane, with a slight distortion of the Greek '*protos*', that is, 'first'; and buthane, with the root of '*butyr*', which in turn takes its origin from a Greek word meaning 'ricotta'. The other saturated hydrocarbons, penthane, hexane, heptane, and so on were named with less imagination and recourse to Greek numerals that correspond to the number of the respective carbon atoms.

A second chemical language, less fanciful but more expressive, is the one composed of the so-called raw formulae. To say that common sugar is $C_{12}H_{22}O_{11}$ or the old piramidon, dear to country practitioners, $C_{13}H_{17}ON_3$, gives us no indication of its origin nor the uses of the two substances, but represents their inventory. It is precisely, a raw, incomplete language: it tells us that to build a molecule of pyramidon thirteen atoms of carbon are needed, seventeen of hydrogen, one of oxygen, three of nitrogen, but it tells us nothing about the order or the structure in which those atoms are linked together. In short, it works as if a typographer extracted from his type font the letters e, a, c, r, and claimed he had in this way expressed the word care: the reader who is not initiated or assisted by the context could also 'read' race, acre, or who knows what other anagram. It is a summary way of writing, which has the sole value (precisely typographical) of fitting neatly into the printed line.

The third language has all the advantages, and only one disadvantage due to the fact that its 'words' do not fit the usual printed line. It tries (or expects) to give us a portrait, an image of the minuscule molecular edifice: it has renounced a good part of the symbolism which is characteristic of all languages, and has regressed to illustration, to pictography. It is as if, instead of the word *acre*, the image of the acre were printed or drawn. The system reminds us of the scholar in the country of the Balnibarbi, about whom Swift speaks in *Gulliver's Travels*: according to him one must reason without speaking and he suggested keeping on hand in place of words 'such things as were necessary to express the particular business they are to discourse on' that is, what today is called the 'referent', a ring if the talk is about rings, a cow if cows are being talked about, and so on. In this way the scholar argued, 'it would serve as a universal language to be understood in all civilised nations'. There is no doubt that the objective, in fact objectist, language of the Balnibarbi and the structural formulas of chemists approach perfection from the point of view of understandability and internationality, but both involve the inconvenience of bulk, as the unhappy compositors of organic chemistry textbooks know only too well.

Naturally, despite its claims to portraiture, and unlike the Balnibarbi, the language of structural formulae, by the very fact of being a true language, has remained partially symbolic. In the first place because its portraits are not life size, but in a 'scale' (that is, in a huge enlargement) of about one to a hundred million. Secondly, because in place of the atoms' shape they contain their graphic symbol, that is, the abbreviation of their name, and because it has proven useful by means of symbolic hyphens between one atom and the next to introduce and represent the forces that hold these atoms together.

Finally, for the fundamental reason which is valid for all portraits, according to which the represented object generally has a thickness, a three-dimensional structure, whereas the portrait is flat because the page on which it is printed is flat. And yet, despite these limitations, if these conventional models are compared with the 'true', almost photographic portraits which can be obtained by subtle techniques for a few decades now, their resemblance is striking: the word-molecules, the little drawings derived from reasoning and experimentation are indeed very similar to the ultimate particles of matter which the ancient atomists had intuited when seeing motes of dust dancing in a beam of sunlight.

# The Language of Chemists (II)

When I was a working chemist I suffered from heat, frost and fear, and I would never have thought that after leaving my old trade, I could feel any nostalgia for it. But it happens, during empty moments, when the human apparatus spins in neutral, like an idling motor: it happens, thanks to the singular filtering power of the mind, which lets happy memories survive and slowly stifles the others. I have recently seen again an old fellow prisoner and we had the usual conversations of veterans: our wives noticed and pointed out to us that in two hours of conversation we had not brought up even a single painful memory, but only the rare moments of remission or the bizarre episodes.

I have before me the table of chemical elements, the 'periodic system', and I am filled with nostalgia, as if I were looking at old school photographs, the boys with their little ties and the girls in their modest black smocks: 'one by one I recognise you all . . .' Of the struggles, defeats and victories that have tied me to certain elements I have already recounted elsewhere; as I also did with their characters, virtues, vices and oddities. But now my trade is a different one, it is the trade of words, chosen, weighed, fitted into a pattern with patience and caution: thus for me also the elements tend to become words, and instead of the thing its name and the why of its name interests me acutely. The panorama is different, but just as varied as that of the things themselves.

Everyone knows that 'proper' elements, those existing in

nature, both on earth and in the stars, are ninety-two, from nitrogen to uranium (actually the latter during the last decades has lost a bit of its good repute). Well, their names, passed in review, constitute a picturesque mosaic which extends in time from far-off prehistory until the present day, and in which appear perhaps all the Western languages and civilisations: our mysterious Indo-European fathers, ancient Egypt, the Greek of the Greeks, the Greek of the Hellenists, the Arab of the alchemists, the nationalistic prides of the past century, right down to the suspect internationalism of this post-war period.

We begin the review with the best known and least exotic elements, nitrogen and sodium. Their international symbols, that is, the single letter or the group of two letters which abbreviate its conventional and original name are respectively N and Na, the initials of Nitrogenium and Natrium, and here comes to light the vestiges of an ancient misunderstanding. Nitrogenium means 'born from nitro', and natrium means 'substance of natro': now, originally, in the language of ancient Egypt *nitro* and *natro* were the same thing.

In the complicated script of that language it was considered superfluous to indicate vowels (perhaps because carving stone is more strenuous than using a ballpoint pen, and cutting down on vowels saved the stonecutters work), and the consonants *ntr* generically indicated saline efflorescences: either that on old walls, which in Italian is still called '*salnitro*', and in other languages, more expressively saltpetre, that is salt of stone or that which the Egyptians extracted from certain quarries and used for mummification: this last is mainly composed of soda. or sodium carbonate, while saltpetre is composed of nitrogen, oxygen and potassium.

Both in brief were 'non-salt salt', substances with a saline appearance, soluble in water, colourless, but with a taste different from that of common salt; and glassmakers soon realised that in the manufacture of glass one could be replaced by the other without a great difference in the end product (which for us is quite understandable: at the temperature of the glassmakers' crucible both salts decompose, the acid part leaves, and in the fused mass only the oxide of the metal remains). The Greeks, and later the Latins, transliterating the Egyptian writing, introduced vowels in accordance with largely arbitrary criteria, and only since then the variant 'nitro' began to indicate specifically saltpetre, the father of Nitrogen, and 'natro', to indicate soda, the mother of Sodium.

For all that, Nitrogen, a chemically rather inert substance, is at the centre of century-old quarrels as regards nomenclature. Baptised in this fashion almost a century ago by a French chemist on the basis of a dubious Hellenism ('the lifeless') it is on the contrary, as said, 'generated by nitro' (nitrogen) for the English-speaking and 'suffocating' (*Stickstoff*) for the Germans. Not even on the symbol is there agreement; the French, who claim its discovery, until a few years ago rejected the N symbol and used a Z in its place: some still use it, polemically.

In running through a list of names of minerals one is confronted by an orgy of personalities. It would seem that no mineralogist was ever resigned to ending his career without linking his name to a mineral, adding to it the ending *-ite* as a laurel wreath: Garnierite, Senarmontite, and thousands of others.

Chemists have always been more discreet; in my review I have found only two names of elements that their discoverers decided to dedicate to themselves and they are Gadolinium (discovered by the Finn Gadolin) and Galium. This last has a curious history. It was isolated in 1875 by the Frenchman Lecocq de Boisbaudrun; '*cocq*' (today written '*coq*') means 'cock' and Lecocq baptised his element 'gallium'. A few years later, in the same mineral examined by the Frenchman the German chemist Winkler discovered a new element; those were years of great tension between Germany and France, the German assumed Gallium to be a nationalistic homage to Gaul and baptised his element Germanium in order to even the score.

Besides these two, only a few personal names have been

given to the newest, unstable and heavier elements than uranium, which have been obtained by man in minimal quantities in nuclear reactors and in the enormous particle accelerators dedicated respectively to Mendeleev, Einstein, Madame Curie, Alfred Noble, and Enrico Fermi.

More than a third of the elements have received names that refer to their most striking properties, arrived at by more or less tortuous linguistic itineraries. So it is for Chloride, Iodine, Chrome, from Greek words which respectively mean green, purple, and colour, and with reference to the colour of the salts or vapours (or, in other cases, to the spectral emission lines). Thus Barium is the 'heavy', Phosphorus is the 'luminous', Bromine and Osmium are, in different degrees, the 'stinkers' (but what chemist worthy of the name could confuse these two most unpleasant odours?).

Still in this spirit which I would call descriptive, and which attests to modesty and good sense, Hydrogen and Oxygen were named, respectively, 'generated by water' and 'by acids'; but since the baptism was performed (or confirmed) by the Frenchman Lavoisier, the German chemists did not consider it valid and imitated it with two approximate translations: *Wasserstoff* and *Sauerstoff*, that is, respectively, 'the substance of water' and 'of acids', and the Russians did the same, coining the couple *Vodorod* and *Kisslorod*.

Only three of the elements which have received 'descriptive' names bear witness to a leap of the imagination: Disprosium ('the impervious'), Lantanium ('the hidden') and Tantalium. In this last denomination, the discoverer (Ekeberg, 1802: he was a Swede, a neutral, and therefore the name chosen by him was not subjected to changes) referred to Tantalus, the mythical sinner described in the *Odyssey*; he is immersed in water up to the neck, but undergoes the agonies of thirst because every time he bends to drink the water recedes, uncovering arid ground. The same ordeal had been suffered by him, the pioneering chemist, in the alternating hopes and disappointments through which he had finally succeeded in discovering his element.

Besides the already mentioned Germanium, about twenty elements have received names that more or less clearly commemorate the country or city in which they were discovered: Lutetium from the ancient name of Paris, Scandium from Scandinavia, Olmium from Stockholm, Renium from the Rhine. Alongside these geographic celebrities attention must be drawn to the obscure village of Ytterby in Sweden because near it a mineral was found which proved to contain numerous unknown elements. The mineral was called Ytterbite and by taking various segments of this last name, with a procedure similar to that of the puzzle-makers' 'logogriphs', Ytterbium, Yttrium, Terbium and Erbium were successively coined.

I have deliberately left aside the history of the veteran elements, known to everyone, characterised and exploited by the most ancient civilisation thousands and thousands of years before the first chemist was born: Iron, Gold, Silver, Copper, Sulphur and several others. It is a complicated and fascinating story, worth being told elsewhere.

# The Book of Strange Data

Just as Francesco Berni dared to write poetry in praise of the plague and urinals, so I dare to declare that inflation too had at least one good aspect, that of making the value of one million clear to everyone: a figure which now, as opposed to the times of Signor Bonaventura (who gave millions away in the 1930s), is within the reach of almost all wallets. In effect, our ability to imagine such a sum is small, and whoever tries to get us to understand how large very large things are, and how small small ones, runs up against an ancient deafness in us, besides the inadequacy of the common language. The popularisers of such sciences as astronomy and nuclear physics have always known this and have tried to make up for this inadequacy by recourse to paradox and proportion: if the sun were reduced to the size of an apple . . ., if a billion years were compressed in a single day . . .

The didactic value of such artifices can vary within very broad limits, and depends, above all, on their elegance: if this is lacking, the reader is again overcome by the same feeling of frustration he experienced when reading the bare data. Challenging these dangers, an old Dutch scientist has with youthful boldness gone up the path of paradox, of sudden comparative illuminations beyond all limits of the absurd, moved by the desire to show how strange the universe around us is, even in those aspects whose strangeness is veiled by habit.

In a book published several years ago but still topical, our R. Houwink (one of the world's best known scholars in the field of polymers and rubber) has given himself the pleasure of gathering several hundred curiosities taken from astronomy, the physics of particles, biology, and economy* which right from its introduction warns us to keep in mind the order of magnitude: the nano-seconds, which are discussed with excessive nonchalance in regard to computers, are brief units of time; there are as many in one second as there are seconds in thirty years.

Astronomy is the domain of 'astronomic numbers', and we all know, at least qualitatively, that the stars are many, but Houwink's image is so much more eloquent and easier to remember: in our galaxy alone every human being who 'wanted to get away' would have the choice of thirty solar systems. Seeing a shooting star seems to us a rather unusual sight, and we are surprised when we are told that the greater part of 'these stars' are in reality metallic or stony granules smaller than a grain of millet; and yet every day Earth receives fifteen thousand tons of them: if this invisible 'dry rain', which probably has continued uninterruptedly since our planet came into existence, were not continually washed down by rains, it would have formed a layer of cosmic dust twenty metres thick.

We are just as unable to conceive of the enormity of the stars as we are the smallness of particles: therefore it is helpful for us to know that a teaspoon of sea water contains as many molecules as there are teaspoonsful contained in the Atlantic Ocean. Electrons rotate around the atomic nuclei at a speed ten times greater than that of the missiles launched by man, but when a conductor with a section of one square millimetre is traversed by a current of one ampere, the electrons advance at a ridiculous speed: twenty-five centimetres an hour, greatly inferior to a queue in front of a post office window. What is the diameter of these electrons? It is practically useless to mention figures to the layman: it is more picturesque to tell him that if Noah in the year 3,000 B.C. had begun to string

* *The Odd Book of Data*, Elsevier, Amsterdam, 1965.

electrons on a thread, one a second, for eight working hours a day, the necklace today would be two tenths of a millimetre long.

It is known that vegetables grow by drawing carbon not from the soil but from the air, and precisely by exploiting carbon dioxide, traces of which are present in the atmosphere, but it is amazing to learn that the carbon fixed thus every year, which is also the only carbon available as food for animals and man, is forty times more abundant than the carbon which in the same period of time is extracted from coal mines.

That the future of mankind rests in the last analysis in the way (rational, irrational or mad) in which the soil is cultivated and cattle are raised, is proven by several illuminating facts. For each human being there exists five hectares of emerged land, but of these one is too cold to be exploited, one too mountainous, one too sterile, and one too arid; that leaves only one hectare per person, but of this, today, only half is cultivated. A single American farmer produces approximately one hundred kilos of grain an hour (but we are not told with what investments); to obtain this result one would require seventeen Chilean farmers, twenty-four Pakistanis, and fifty Japanese: comparison data for Italy and other European countries are not given. A Danish cow produces each year ten times its own weight in milk; an Indian cow only twice its weight, but, since it is very skinny, in absolute terms it yields one-tenth of the Danish cow's milk.

It is probable that certain numerical coincidences are not the product of chance: it is calculated that on the surface of a fertile pasture the weight of bacteria that exists per hectare is the same as the weight of the cattle that the pasture can maintain. A cubic centimetre of this soil contains a number of micro-organisms comparable to the world's human population: which sufficiently pressed together would fit in Lake Windermere in England (approximately the size of our Lake d'Orta).

To the disappointment of the adherents of macrobiotics and the consolation of the hungry, we hear that in the United

States seventeen volunteers were fed for several months exclusively with foods obtained by synthesis, that is, by chemical means, excluding all products of vegetable and animal origin; at the end of the experiment all these subjects were in excellent health. Hence a factory of modest dimensions would be sufficient to feed a large city. The news reassures us only in part. We would like to know the result of such an experiment over a greater length of time, because diseases due to privation take some time to appear.

Seen through Houwink's lens our body acquires surreal features, now ether, now clay. A woman resting her weight on her spiked heel exerts upon the ground a pressure similar to that of a high pressure steam generator; the current of air which runs through our nose in a normal inhalation corresponds to a No. 2 wind-force on the Beaufort scale; but the energies employed by our auxiliary services (the organs of sensation and communication) are incredibly low. The sum of energy expended by an average man speaking three hours a day all his life long would be barely sufficient to heat a cup of tea, and the energy that could be extracted from a pea falling from a height of three centimetres, if wholly converted into luminous energy, would be sufficient to stimulate the optical nerves of all the human beings who have existed until now.

Our brain is the most complex object existing in the universe, but no more energy is required for it to function than for a hundred watt bulb. To this statement we can add that just as for the bulb, the greater part of this energy is dissipated in heat, the amount actually utilised for mental operations is minimal, and so far as I know up until now it has not been measured.

Each one of the data drawn from the field of economics is a small electric shock. A dollar invested at a compound interest of one percent a year since the birth of Christ would today have the same value as one hundred thousand terrestrial globes of solid gold. At any rate, it is by now incorrect to refer to gold as the precious substance par excellence: plutonium is worth thirty times more, and neutrons a million times. However, if I am allowed a personal observation, I would take the liberty of advising against a hoarding of these two materials; plutonium is radioactive and very toxic, and neutrons would be a very bad investment because they have a fission time of approximately sixty minutes. This is the same as saying that anyone who were to buy a kilogram of neutrons would be left five hundred grams after a quarter of an hour, two hundred and fifty grams after half an hour, one hundred and twenty-five after forty minutes, and so on.

Our consumer civilisation is in actuality a civilisation of wasters. An office employee 'produces' today two kilograms of wastepaper a day which contains more calories than are needed to keep him and his wife. In the industrialised countries, the trucks that are scrapped have not lost one per thousandth of their weight. In terms of ink and fuel respectively a kilometre written with a ballpoint pen and a kilometre travelled by car cost approximately the same, if one leaves aside the wages of the driver and the writer.

The book describes approximately two hundred items of this kind. Some are elegant, or frivolous, or grotesque, but not one is useless: they are all meant to help us understand the world in which we live, that is, give us a concrete notion of it, but in many cases 'to understand' instead means to realise that with certain objects and phenomena we are not able to form an image (the same happens with God, according to certain religions). Our imagination has our dimensions and we cannot demand that it exceed them. Classical physics, too, has our dimensions; to descend into the core of atoms, or rise into intergalactic space a different physics is necessary, which intuition no longer aids but in fact impedes. For laymen like us the only instrument that allows us to cast a glance beyond our borders are 'the odd data'. They are not science but a stimulus to acquire it.

# Writing a Novel

After thirty-five years of apprenticeship and camouflaged or open 'autobiographism', I decided one day to step over the embankment and try to write a novel without paying too much attention to the on-going polemic as to whether the novel is alive or dead, and, if alive, whether it is in good health. Now that the enterprise is accomplished, and the book printed and in the bookstores, I have the agreeable impression of returning from an exotic trip, and like all those who return, I want to tell about the things I've seen and 'show the slides' to friends. It is well known that sometimes during those unasked-for exhibitions friends get bored; if so, in this case they have only to turn the page.

What does one feel when writing about invented things? Writing about things seen is easier than inventing, and less joyful. It is writing-describing: you have a trail, you dig into your close or distant memories, put the specimens in order (if you have a talent for it), catalogue them, then you pick up a kind of mental camera and snap: you can be a mediocre, good, or even 'artistic' photographer; you can ennoble the things you portray, or report them in an impersonal, modest, and honest manner, or on the contrary give them a distorted, flat, un-focused, off-centre, under- or over-exposed image, but in every case you are guided, held by the hand by the facts, you have ground under your feet.

Writing a novel is different, it is super-writing: you are no longer on the ground, you fly, with all the emotions, fears and enthusiasms of a pioneer in a bi-plane made of canvas, string and plywood; or better, in an anchored balloon whose mooring line has been cut. The first sensation, destined to be reduced later on to smaller dimensions, is one of unlimited, almost licentious freedom. You can choose whichever subject or event you wish, tragic, fantastic or comic, lunar, solar, or saturnine; you can situate it in a time that runs from the First Day of Creation (or even before, why not?) until today, indeed the remotest future, which you are entitled to mould at your will. You can set your story where you wish: in the living room of your own house, the empyrean, the court of Tamerlane, the hold of a fishing boat, inside a red blood cell, at the bottom of a mine, or in a brothel: in short, in any place you have seen or in places you've heard described, or read about, or seen at the movies or in a photograph, or imagined, imaginary, imaginable, unimaginable.

All of the Earth is yours, indeed the cosmos; and if the cosmos seems tight to you, you can invent another that suits you. If it obeys the laws of physics and common sense, fine; if not, fine all the same, or perhaps even better; in any case, you will not unleash catastrophe, at the most some picayune reader will write you to express urbanely his disappointment or his dissent. In short, aside from the time you'll have wasted, the risk you run is not greater than that of the student writing an essay in class: at the worst, you'll get a bad mark. Isn't this a wonderful trade?

When it comes to the characters, things become a bit more complicated. On this theme, the *ménage à trois* among author, character, and reader, tons of books have been written, but since I have now become a member of the crew, I take the liberty of giving you a piece of my mind, that is, showing my slides. Where the characters are concerned, one has at the beginning the impression of a boundless freedom. In the abstract you have an absolute power over them, such as no tyrant on the face of the earth ever had. You can give them life, as dwarfs or giants, you can afflict them, torture them, kill them, resurrect them; or give them the gift of beauty and eternal youth, strength, the wisdom you do not have, the happiness of every moment (but will you be able to describe this without boring your reader?), love, wealth, and genius. But only in the abstract, because you are tied to them more than it may seem.

Every one of these phantasms is born from you, has your blood, for good or evil. It is your bloom. Worse, it is a spy assigned to you, reveals a part of you, your tensions, like those glass tassels that are used to reveal whether a crack in the wall is bound to grow wider. They are your way of saying 'I': when you make them move or speak, reflect on what you are doing for they might say too much. Perhaps they will live longer than you, perpetuating your vices and errors.

The characters of a book are in truth strange creatures. They have neither skin nor blood nor flesh, they have less reality than a painting or a nocturnal dream, they have no substance but words, black doodles on a white sheet of paper. and yet you pass the time with them, converse with them through the centuries, hate them, love them, fall in love with them. Every one of them is a depository of certain rights, and knows how to enforce them, have them recognised. Your freedom as author is only apparent. If, having once conceived your homunculus, you thwarted it, if you want to impose on him a gesture contrary to his nature, or forbid him an act which will be congenial to him, you meet with resistance, muted but indubitable: as if you tried to command your hand to touch a red-hot iron or an object which repels you (or it). He, the non-existent, is there – he is, he weighs, pushes against your hand: wants and does not want, silent and stubborn. If you persevere, he becomes morose. He withdraws, ceases to collaborate with you, to prompt you with his lines; he loses body, becomes flat, thin, white. He is paper and turns back into paper.

There is also another way in which your freedom of invention is apparent. Just as it is impossible to transform a real person into a character, that is, fashion an objective undistorted biography of him, so it is impossible to perform the reverse operation, to coin a character without pouring into it not only your moods as the author but also fragments of people you have met or of other characters.

The first impossibility is demonstrated by thousands of years of literature. The success of the written portrait is always limited, even in the best texts: the entire *Odyssey* is not enough to give us the image of Ulysses, but not even in the novel in the classic mode, or in the straight biography, where the author strives to describe for you the height of his subject, the colour of his hair, eyes, and complexion, the shape of his body, his way of speaking, laughing, gesticulating: not even here, ever, due to the essential inadequacy of our expressive means, is nemesis attained. The movies and television attain it with closer approximation; in fact the filmed takes of dead people move us to a much greater degree than written portraits. They perturb us: the man whom we see move and speak on the screen really is not completely dead. And if holograms will make us the gift of a third dimension, our perturbation will be enormously greater, it will strike us as black magic. Trying to compete with such media is, for a writer, a waste of time.

But the impossibility of creating a character from nothing seems to me just as iron-clad. I already said that inevitably the author transfers into it (knowingly or not, willingly or not, sometimes becoming aware of it only when rereading his pages years after having written them) a part of himself; but the rest, the not-self, is never completely invented. It swarms with memories: these too, conscious or unconscious, voluntary or not. The character that you naïvely believe you have manufactured in your workshop reveals itself to be a chimera, a mosaic of tesserae, of shots snapped at some mysterious time and relegated to the attic of memory. In short a conglomerate that you will have the merit to have brought to life and made credible; but I do not believe that one can lay down rules for this art of producing an organism from a pile of odds and ends.

One can enunciate negative rules; it is not necessary for your character to be virtuous, attractive, or wise; nor is it necessary for him to be consistent with himself, indeed perhaps the contrary is true. The too consistent character is predictable, that is, boring: he does not have impulses, he is programmed, he doesn't have free will. He must be inconsistent as we all are, have changing moods, make mistakes, get lost, grow from page to page, or fade away: if he remains the same he will not be the simulacrum of a creature but the simulacrum of a statue, that is, a double simulacrum.

Of course, beneath this inconsistency there is a deeper consistency, but to define it is beyond my abilities; whether it has been respected one knows afterwards when the page is written, and the signal is given by the reader's blood which for a few minutes circulates a trifle warmer and a trifle faster.

# François Rabelais

Some books are dear to us without our being able to say exactly why: in such cases, by carrying our investigation just a bit deeper, it is probable that unsuspected affinities could be discovered, rich in revelations as regards the least obvious aspects of our character. But other books accompany us for years, for life, and the reason is clear, accessible, easy to express in words: among these, with reverence and love, I dare to mention *Gargantua and Pantagruel*, the colossal but only work by Rabelais, '*mon maître*'. The strange fate of this book is known: born from the love of life and cultivated leisure of Rabelais, this monk, physician, philologist, traveller and humanist, it grew and proliferated with an absolute lack of plan for almost twenty years and more than one thousand pages, accumulating the most extravagant inventions in full imaginative freedom, half a robust popular epic of buffoonery, half imbued with the vigorous and vigilant moral consciousness of a great Renaissance spirit. On each page we encounter, daringly juxtaposed, inspired, ribald, or jejune scurrilities, and at the same time quotations (authentic and not, almost all quoted from memory) from Latin, Greek, Arabic, and Hebrew texts; dignified and resonant, oratorical exercises; Aristotelian subtleties that give rise to gigantic laughter, while others are endorsed and validated with the good faith of a man whose life is pure.

If to this fundamentally discontinuous texture and its frequent linguistic difficulties one adds the violent criticisms and satires directed against the Roman Curia, it is easy to understand why at all times *Gargantua and Pantagruel* has found a limited audience, and why it has been tried to pass it off, opportunely amputated and reshaped, as children's literature. And yet I only have to open it to find in it the book of today, I mean the book of all times, eternal, which speaks a language that will always be understood.

It isn't that in it the fundamental themes of the human comedy are dealt with: on the contrary one would look in vain for the great traditional poetic sources, love, death, religious experience, precarious fate. In Rabelais there is no morose retreat into oneself, rethinking, inner searching: in every word of his there lives a different state of soul, fanciful, extrovert, substantially that of the innovator, the inventor (not the Utopian); the inventor of large and small things, and also that of the 'bosin', the extemporaneous 'barker' at a country fair. At any rate it is not a chance return; it is known that the book had an obscure precursor, which disappeared for centuries without a trace: a country fair almanac, *Chroniques du grand Géant Gargantua*. But the two giants of his dynasty are not only mountains of flesh, absurd drinkers and eaters: together, and paradoxically, they are the legitimate epigones who declared war on Jupiter, sprang from Nimrod and Goliath, and are at once enlightened princes and joyous philosophers. In Pantagruel's vast inspiration and vast laughter is enclosed the dream of the century, that of an industrious and productive humanity which turns its back on the darkness and resolutely walks towards a future of peaceful prosperity, towards the golden age described by the Latins, neither past nor distantly future but within reach, provided the powerful of the earth do not abandon the path of reason and remain strong against external and internal enemies.

This is not an idyllic hope, it is a robust certainty. It is enough to want it and the world will be yours: it is enough to have education, justice, science, art, the laws, and the example of the ancients. God exists, but in the heavens: man is free, not predestined, he is '*faber sui*', and must and can dominate the earth, the divine gift. Therefore the world is beautiful, it is full of joy, not tomorrow but today: because to each person are available the illustrious joys of virtue and knowledge, and also the bodily joys, they too a divine gift, of dizzily overflowing tables, 'theological' drunks, and indefatigable sensual pleasures. To love men means to love them as they are, body and soul, '*tripes et boyaux*'.

Panurge, the only character in the book who has human dimensions and never trespasses into symbol and allegory, is an extraordinary hero in reverse, a condensation of a restless and curious humanity in whom much more than in Pantagruel Rabelais seems to be sketching himself, his modern man's complexity, his contradictions, unresolved and gaily accepted. Panurge, charlatan, pirate, '*clerc*', turn by turn hoaxer and hoaxed, full of courage, 'except when in danger', famished, penniless and dissolute, who appears on the scene begging for bread in all living and dead languages, Panurge is us, man. He is not exemplary, he is not 'perfection', but he is humanity, alive because it seeks, sins, enjoys and knows.

How is this intemperate, pagan, terrestrial doctrine reconciled with the evangelical message, never denied nor forgotten by Rabelais' shepherd of souls? It is not reconciled at all: this too is intrinsic to the human condition of being suspended between the mire and the heavens, between nothing and the infinite. Rabelais' very life, as far as one knows, is a tangle of contradictions, a maelstrom of activities apparently incompatible with each other and with the image of the author as it is traditionally reconstructed from his writings.

A Franciscan monk, then (at the age of forty) a student of medicine and physician at the Lyons Hospital, publisher of scientific books and popular almanacs, scholar of jurisprudence, Greek, Arabic and Hebrew, indefatigable traveller, astrologist, botanist, archaeologist, the friend of Erasmus, the precursor of Vesalius in the study of anatomy on the human corpse: author among the freest, he is at the same time the curate of Meudon. Throughout his life he enjoyed the reputation of a pious and irreproachable man; yet he leaves behind him (deliberately, one would say) the portrait of a sensual man, if not a satyr. We are far from, we are at the antipodes of the stoic wisdom of the golden mean. The Rabelesian teaching is extremist, it is the virtue of excess: not only are Gargantua and Pantagruel giants but the book itself is a giant, both as regards size and scope; gigantic and fabulous are the exploits, the revelries, the diatribes, the manhandling of mythology and history, the lists of words.

Gigantic above every other thing is Rabelais' and his creatures' capacity for joy. This boundless and luxuriating epic of satisfied flesh unexpectedly reaches heaven by a different route: because the man who feels joy is like the man who feels love, he is good, he is grateful to his Creator for having created him, and therefore he will be saved. For the rest, the carnality described by the extremely erudite Rabelais is so naïve and natural as to disarm every intelligent censor: it is healthy and innocent and as irresistible as are the forces of nature.

Why is Rabelais close to us? He certainly does not resemble us, indeed he is rich in all the virtues that today's man, sad, shackled, and weary, lacks. He is close to us as a model. Because of his merrily curious spirit, his amiable scepticism, his faith in tomorrow and in man; and also because of his way of writing, so alien to genres and rules. Perhaps we can trace back to him and his Abbey of Thelma that manner, which is triumphant today and so evident in Sterne and Joyce, of 'writing as you please', without codes or precepts, following the thread of imagination, just as out of spontaneous necessity a carnival procession winds along, different and surprising at every turn. He is close to us, chiefly because in this boundless painter of terrestrial joys we perceive the permanent, firm consciousness matured through many experiences that not all of life is here. It would be difficult to find a single melancholy page in all of his work, and yet Rabelais knows human misery; he is silent about it because, also a good physician when he writes, he does not accept it, he wants to heal it:

*Mieulx est de ris que de larmes escrire*
*Pour ce que rire est le propre de l'homme.*

# The Force of Amber

If one rubs amber with a cloth, small, curious phenomena are produced: one hears a crackling, in the dark one sees sparks, small bits of straw and specks of paper brought close dance about madly. In Greek, amber is called *electron*; until around 1600 these effects had not been observed on other substances, and therefore they have been called electrical effects. To give a name to a thing is as gratifying as giving a name to an island, but it is also dangerous: the danger consists in one's becoming convinced that all is taken care of and that once named the phenomenon has also been explained.

Now nobody, until well into the nineteenth century, had suspected that this little trick with amber was a sign to decipher: that it was the annunciation by enigma of a force that would change the face of the world, and that the graceful sparks shared the nature of a lightning bolt. Nevertheless all Western languages have preserved the term 'electricity', that is 'the force of amber': only the Hungarians have coined a neologism which says, more logically, the 'force of the lightning bolts'.

Today everyone knows that electrical effects are obtained by rubbing certain solid bodies against each other, but little emphasis is put on the fact that analogous phenomena are also produced by the attrition of a liquid against a solid. I found out about this many years ago in a dramatic way.

It was summer. In the yard of the factory there stood a tank which contained ten tons of a solvent. A worker went up to it holding a receptacle: he meant to fill it, as he and others had done innumerable times. He turned the tank's spigot and the solvent poured out in flames, as from a flame thrower. The worker threw away the receptacle and ran to sound the alarm. Meanwhile the liquid continued to flow: a burning puddle had formed on the ground and was rapidly spreading and threatened to invade the production section.

The situation was saved by a brave and experienced man who by chance was on the spot (to everyone's great good fortune): he managed to squeeze between the flames and the tank and close the spigot, after which the fire burnt itself out without causing much damage. This spontaneous igniting of a quite common substance seemed mysterious and magical, but afterwards I found its explanation in a specialised textbook: indeed, certain liquids, very pure hydrocarbons among them, become electrified when flowing through a conduit at a speed over certain limits.

Between that tank and the spigot there was in fact a stretch of rather thin pipe; the worker must have opened the spigot abruptly and the liquid had become electrified along its brief passage. That was the first time the solvent was drawn off that day, but it was already late and there was the sun; hence the liquid had stayed for quite a while in the tube and had the time to become heated beyond its point of flammability. There must have been a small spark, perhaps between the spigot and the liquid itself and the combustion had taken place.

A subtle danger therefore: not obvious, not banal. How could we protect ourselves from it? According to the text mentioned, there exist substances which, added to hydrocarbons in minimal doses, make them sufficiently conductive to eliminate the risks due to 'the force of amber'. It seemed to us strange and absurd that these notions are not better known, even among those who handle solvents; at any rate, we used the prescribed additive, and since then, whether due to it or not, nothing of the kind has happened again.

But on another occasion I myself almost unleashed this

force, because of an excess of zeal and ignorance. It was the morning of 31 December and the factory was closed. The custodian telephoned me to rush over; on the road, in front of the entrance, a trailer full of gasoline had overturned and he did not know what to do. I told him to call the firemen and for good measure I set off too, bracing myself for an unusual New Year's Eve.

I found a sinister scenario. The truck driver, out of prudence or fear, had uncoupled the front section, which was also loaded with gas, and had disappeared into the fog with it. The trailer lay on its side in the street across from the factory, and from the access hatch (which wasn't well shut or had become unbolted because of the impact) gas gushed out. It was very cold and instead of evaporating the gas was spreading over the nearby meadow. Soon after, the firemen arrived; we had a consultation, the first thing to do was lift the trailer but we needed a crane; they called their headquarters to ask for the crane, but I said that lifting the trailer in that atmosphere saturated with gas vapors seemed dangerous to me: the impact of iron against iron could produce sparks. At that the firemen proposed to cover everything with foam, the trailer, the street and the meadow, and this was done in a flash so that the meadow became snow-white and was a beautiful sight.

While we were waiting for the crane and while the gas continued to pour out, slipping under the foam cover, the thought of another danger struck me. As the tank emptied, air entered and replaced the gas, but that air became saturated with flammable vapours: an explosive mixture could form and one could not exclude the possibility of sparks being produced for one reason or another due to the lifting operations, the impact of a monkey wrench, or the very attrition of the gas that was pouring out: who knows whether it contained the famous additive?

I told the chief of the firemen that it would be a good idea to fill the air vacuum with inert gas. In the factory we had many carbon dioxide fire extinguishers: we could carefully lift the hatch, introduce the dioxide and shut it again. The lieutenant approved; it was night by now and we began the operation with illumination from the floodlights. One after the other we unloaded into half of the tank (the other half was still full of gas which, due to the vehicle's inclined position could not continue to flow out) five or six extinguishers, then we shut the hatch again.

Meanwhile the cold had grown more intense and the fog thicker; the rest of the world in the warmth of their houses were preparing for the New Year's Eve festivities, and we felt abandoned. The firemen ran like tight-rope artists up and down the rubber hose of the foam generator, because the mixture it contained was freezing. The overturned trailer, blanketed in foam, had taken on the appearance of a century-old wreck.

At last the crane arrived, shortly before midnight, and with it arrived some champagne offered, I no longer remember by whom, whether by the firemen, the oil company, or the factory. The trailer was lifted up, we pounded each others' shoulders with joy and also to warm up a bit, and drank to the New Year, the success of the operation, and the danger we had avoided.

Two days later I learned that the danger we had escaped was more serious than we imagined. In another book, known just as little, I read that carbon dioxide extinguishers are excellent for putting out fires in progress, but must absolutely not be used for preventive purposes in the presence of flammable solvents. The carbon dioxide, violently issuing from the nozzle, cools and condenses into needles of 'dry ice'; these needles, rubbing against the nozzle, become electrified and generate sparks which can ignite the solvent before the atmosphere becomes inert, or when the extinguisher is empty. The book described a ruinous fire and explosion which took place in Holland: dozens of people had died, and it had been unleashed precisely by the improper use of a carbon dioxide extinguisher.

It seems to me that a moral can be drawn from these two episodes. Our world is becoming ever more complicated and each of us needs an ever more refined and up-to-date competence. There are many dangerous trades, and the analysis of the dangers (manifest and hidden) should constitute the ABCs of every professional training course. It will never be possible to eliminate all risk nor to solve all problems, but every solved problem is a victory in terms of saved human lives, health and wealth.

Competence has no surrogates: we have seen this recently in the terrible episode of the boy who fell into an abandoned well and died after two days of generous but mistaken attempts to save him. Goodwill, courage, the spirit of sacrifice, extemporaneous ingenuity are not much help, indeed, in the absence of competence they can be harmful. To men of goodwill is promised peace on earth, but, in emergency situations, woe to those who trust rescuers who have only goodwill at their disposal.

# The Irritable Chess-Players

Horace, himself a poet, already confessed that he let many things pass rather than make an enemy of the irritable genus of poets; and poets, or more generally writers, are irritable still: it is enough to think of the events surrounding literary prizes and the visceral hatred with which the poet showers the critic when his review contains only the shadow of a doubt. We now read, while at Merano Karpov and Korchnoy are silently tearing each other limb from limb, how irritable chess players are. Why is this quality shared by chess players and poets? Do chess and poetry have anything in common?

The adepts of the noble game claim that it is so: a game of chess, even if played by dilettantes, is an austere metaphor of life and a struggle for life, and the chess player's virtues – reason, memory and invention – are the virtues of every thinking man. The stern rule of chess, according to which the piece that was touched must be moved, and it is not permissible to re-do a move of which one repents, reproduces the inexorability of the choices of the living. When your king, as a result of your inexperience, lack of attention, imprudence, or the opponent's superiority, is ever more closely threatened (but the threat must be enunciated in a clear voice, it is never insidious), cornered, and finally transfixed, you cannot fail to perceive a symbolic shadow beyond the chess board. You are living a death; it is your death, and at the same time it is a death for which you are guilty. Living it, you exorcise it and strengthen yourself.

So this chivalrous and ferocious game is poetic; it is felt as such by all those who have practised it at whatever level, but I believe that the cause for the irritability of poets and chess players is not to be found here. Poets, and anyone who ever exercises a creative and individual profession, have in common with chess players total responsibility for their actions. This happens rarely, or does not happen at all in other human activities, whether they be paid and serious or unpaid and playful. Perhaps it is not by chance that tennis players, for example, who play alone or at most in pairs, are more irascible and neurotic than soccer players or cyclists, who work in teams.

Whoever is on his own, without allies or intermediaries between himself and his work, has no excuses in the face of failure, and excuses are a precious analgesic. The actor can unload the blame of a failure on his director, or vice versa; someone who works in an industry feels his responsibility diluted in that of numerous colleagues, superiors and inferiors, and moreover contaminated by 'contingency', competition, the whims of the market and the unforeseen. Someone who teaches can blame the programmes, the dean, and of course the student.

The political man, at least in a pluralistic regime, gets ahead through a thicket of tensions, collusions, evident or hidden hostilities, traps, and favours, and when he fails he has a thousand opportunities to justify himself with others and himself; but the despot, the repository of absolute power, totally answerable by his open and admitted choice when faced by collapse looks for someone to answer for him: he too wants the analgesic. Hitler himself, in the besieged Chancellery, one hour before killing himself, wild with rage unloaded all his misdeeds on the German people who had not been worthy of him. But the person who decides to attack with the bishop the point he considers weak in his opponent's deployment, is alone, he has no co-responsibles, not even putative, and fully and singly answers for his decision, like the poet at his writing table faced by 'the tiny verse'. Even if only a game is involved, he is adult and mature.

It must be added that poet and chess player work only with their brain, and when it comes to the quality of our brain we are all very touchy. To accuse another of having weak kidneys, lungs, or heart, is not a crime; on the contrary, saying he has a weak brain is a crime. To be considered stupid and to be told so is more painful than being called gluttonous, mendacious, violent, lascivious, lazy, cowardly: every weakness, every vice, has found its defenders, its rhetoric, its ennoblement and exaltation, but stupidity hasn't.

'Stupid' is a strong word and a burning insult: perhaps this is the reason why in all languages and above all in dialects, the term has a myriad of synonyms more or less euphemistic, as is the case with words connected with sex and death. If Christ, according to the Gospel of Matthew (5.22), had thought it proper to warn that anyone who calls his brother *'raca'* (foolish) will be subjected to judgement, and anyone who calls him crazy will go down among the damned, it is clear that he recognised the wounding nature of these expressions. The chess player and the poet are without defence against them: they have laid themselves bare. Every verse of theirs, every move, has their signature. They have no collaborator-accomplices: they did indeed have teachers, in the flesh or at a distance of continents and centuries, but they know that it is cowardice to blame our teachers or at any rate others for our weaknesses. Now, someone who is naked, his skin bared and finely dotted with open nerve ends, without armour to protect him, nor clothes to screen and mask him, is vulnerable and irritable. This is a condition to which in our complicated society we are rarely exposed, yet few are the lives in which the moment of being laid bare doesn't occur. Then we suffer because of the nudity to which we have not adjusted: even the true, non-metaphoric skin becomes irritated if it is exposed to the sun.

For this reason I, an execrable chess player, think it would be a good thing if the game of chess had greater popularity, and was perhaps even taught and practised in the schools, as has been done for a long time in the Soviet Union. In short, it would be a good thing if everybody, and especially those who aspire to command or to a political career, precociously learn to live like chess players, that is, meditating before moving, even though knowing that the time allowed for each move is limited; remembering that every move of ours provokes another by the opponent, difficult but not impossible to foresee; and paying for wrong moves.

The exercise of these virtues is certainly advantageous in the long run, both for the individual and the community. In the short run, it has its price, which is to make us a bit irritable.

# Renzo's Fist

I confess it not with pride, indeed with shame: my appetite for new books grows less and less, and I tend to reread the ones I already know. In the same way, with the passing of the years, the desire (or ability?) to make new friendships decreases, and one prefers to deepen the old friendships; noticing perhaps a few more wrinkles or, instead, a few virtues which one had not been aware of before.

The successive readings of an already familiar book can take place, so to speak, with ever-expanding enlargements, like certain very beautiful sequences of photographs in which one sees a fly, then its head with delicate antennae and multiple eyes, then a single eye like a crystal cupola, and finally the eye's complicated yet necessary inner structure; or the same readings can take place, if we still want to draw on photographic language, with a different lighting or from a different visual angle. To tell the truth, not all books lend themselves to being read with a magnifying glass: in other words, not all have a 'fine structure'; but for those that do have it, the effort is well spent, and these are the books I prefer.

I had just finished re-reading the famous scene in Manzoni's novel *The Betrothed* where Renzo, having recovered from the plague, returns to Milan to search for Lucia. These are splendid pages, sure, rich with a strong and sad human wisdom, which enriches you and which you feel is valid for all times: not only for those in which the story unfolds but for Manzoni's times and for ours. After much useless questioning, Renzo at last learns the address of the house where Lucia supposedly can be found, but he does not feel relief, on the contrary he is deeply troubled: at that definitive moment faced by the immediate and crude alternative – Lucia alive or Lucia dead – 'he would have preferred to be still in the dark about everything, to be at the beginning of the journey, which by now was coming to an end.' Hasn't everyone felt a similar anxiety before the door of a doctor's office? But only an acute observer of the human soul knows how to condense it in a few words and give us back the truth.

Immediately after, in the famous concise episode (little more than a page) of the mother who refuses to entrust to the *monatti* her dead little girl – 'but nicely arranged ... as if adorned for a festive occasion' – and whom she herself places on the cart, there is sketched the greatest of the doubts which afflict religious spirits, the problem of problems, the reason for evil. This is the enigma over which Job and Ivan Karamazov tormented themselves, and it is the blackest stain on Hitler's Germany: why the innocent? why the children? why does providence halt before human wickedness and the world's pain and sorrow? This suggested and unexpressed meditation, this moment of lofty compassion, outlined against the grim background of Milan's streets depopulated by the plague; here the only sign of life is the menacing and sinister presence of the *monatti*: 'some in a red uniform, others ... with plumes and pompoms of various colours which those wretches wore almost as a sign of merriment amid so much public mourning.'

Like the devils of Malebolge the *monatti* are a group; they have developed a group philosophy and morality. Their conversation with Renzo who has found safety on their cart and whom they mistake for an 'anointer', a plague-spreader, is memorable: 'You've come to put yourself under the protection of the *monatti*: it is as good as being in church'; 'you're right to infect this rabble ... who, to reward us for this miserable life of ours ... go around saying that, after the dying is over, they want to hang us all'; shortly before, when Don Rodrigo, struck by the plague, fights against being carried off, a *monatto* shouts at him with rage and contempt: 'Ah, you scoundrel! Attack the *monatti*, eh! Attack the servants of the Tribunal! Attack those who are doing the work of mercy!' They look for justification in other people's eyes and their own: they are 'public officials,' indispensable and above criticism.

It is strange how Manzoni, so felicitous in creating images and metaphors, so precise in depicting states of the soul and landscapes (indeed, the states of the soul are inscribed in the landscapes), becomes so uncertain and awkward when it is a matter of describing the human gesture. I do not know whether this observation is new, nor even if it is justified, but, precisely in the episode mentioned above and on a single page I find two 'gestures' which are just barely credible, or even possible. Renzo, encircled by a crowd of threatening passers-by, pushes his way through and escapes – 'at a gallop, his fist in the air, tight, knuckled, ready for whoever else might get in his way'. Now, it is completely unnatural to run while holding one's fist in the air. It is hampering, even for a few steps: it results in a greater waste of time than would be needed to clench and raise the fist a second time. A graceful Tuscan expression comes to mind: 'A mother on the balcony says to her neighbour: "Signora, since your mouth is already open, would you call my Johnny, who is also down there in the courtyard?"'

Immediately after fleeing Renzo decides to hide on one of the *monatti*'s carts: 'He takes aim, leaps: he's up, standing on his right foot, his left foot in the air, and his arms raised.' This is truly an unsuccessful snapshot, in fact it is invented. In none of the phases of a leap can there be a statuesque stance like the one described here: but perhaps this is more obvious to us, accustomed since childhood to sports' photographs, than to Manzoni's contemporaries.

There are other images like this in the novel, unreal, mannered; they make one think of an indirect mental process, as if the author faced by an attitude of the human body, strove to construct an illustration in keeping with the taste of the times, and then, in the written text, tried to illustrate the illustration itself instead of the immediate visual datum. Renzo, gripped by rage, unusual for him but fully justified by Don Abbondio's reticence, is holding the priest in his room. He wants to learn from him the name of the tyrant who opposes the marriage, 'and he stood bent over, with his ear close to his mouth, his arms stretched behind him and his fists clenched.'

The rendition of the gesture is precise, but the gesture is not very plausible, but rather rhetorical, excessive. It recalls the expressive code of the silent movies, which for us today is bizarre and comical but in its time was accepted by everyone; it was, precisely, a code, fruit of a convention, in accordance with which the gesture was delegated to replace the word which the screen was not yet able to transmit to the spectator and could therefore be very different from everyday gestures.

Renzo, badly advised by Agnes, is on his way to Dr Azzeccagarbugli, and as a token of precautionary homage brings him four capons, since one must never call 'on such gentlemen' with empty hands. In the economy of the page these capons are important and are treated with a discreet and masterful hand. They had been fattened for the nuptial banquet: 'Take those four capons, poor things! whose necks I was going to wring for Sunday's banquet.' That expression 'poor things!' bears the seal of literary and psychological genius: it sums up and embraces that tangle of compassion, tolerance and cynicism which is so typically Italian. The capons are not to be pitied because their necks will be wrung: this is their unquestionable fate as domestic victims. No, Agnes has carried out a transference and recognized in them a symbolic value – the capons are the innocents who suffer for the sins of others: not they but Lucia and Renzo and she herself are the 'poor things'. Not by chance a few sentences further on, they are explicitly humanised, in a comparison which is justly famous and has become proverbial: while Renzo holds them, shaking them roughly, their dangling heads 'contrived to peck each other, as happens only too often among the companions of misfortune'.

But here too in this text exemplary for its pessimistic clair-voyance the human gesture is artificial: even in times of famine four capons weigh at least twenty-four pounds, and only a Hercules could have waved them about, lifted and shook them with only one hand as here described; and what was needed was a Hercules who was an actor and mime instead of a meek silk weaver.

In his introduction to *The Betrothed* in the Einaudi edition, Alberto Moravia suggests that we should see in it a 'Catholic realism' parallel to the 'Socialist realism' of the Soviets, that is, superior literary craftsmanship subservient to the aims of propa-ganda even if often, by its very excellence, the craftsmanship transcends and cancels the aims. This thesis leaves me per-plexed, but certainly the descriptions of some gestures might confirm it.

In Chapter VI, Fra Cristoforo grows indignant over Don Rodrigo's insolence: having been asked to desist from his intrigues against Lucia, Don Rodrigo has suggested that she should be induced to put herself under his protection. '"Your protection!" exclaimed [Fra Cristoforo], taking two steps backward, proudly shifting his weight to his right foot, his right hand on his hip, lifting his left hand with his index finger pointed at Don Rodrigo and transfixing him with a pair of blazing eyes: "Your protection!"' here the Friar is gone and we have the Friar's baroque monument. Once again one must say that the author has arrived at the image by an indirect route: not passing directly from representation to words, but interposing between them a scene played by an actor, and why not admit it, a ham actor at that.

One notes with curiosity that a few pages further on a very similar gesticulation is attributed to Renzo, with a completely different purpose. In the presence of Lucia and Agnes, Renzo, beside himself with rage, has threatened to take justice into his own hands at the cost of losing Lucia's love: the two women try to calm him down. 'Now he remained immobile and pensive for a while, contemplating Lucia's imploring face;

then, all of a sudden, he looked at her grimly, stepped back, lifted his arm, pointed his index finger at her, and shouted: "Her! Yes, it's her he wants. He must die!"' This is probably the least felicitous piece of dialogue in the novel: one has the impression that the theatrical gesture has contaminated the 'soundtrack', dragging it along afterwards.

But here Manzoni is justified: it might be useful for Renzo at that moment to instil fear in Lucia who until then had rejected the hasty solution of a marriage by trickery. Renzo might perhaps have 'used a bit of artifice to make [Lucia's fear] grow, to make it bear fruit'. Manzoni seems willing to admit certain recitative solutions only 'when two passions clamour in a man's heart'; but in that 'clamour' one clearly reads the author's stoic Catholic aversion for the passions by which the character, loved though he may be, is enslaved.

As one can see, reading with a magnifying glass is a pitiless exercise. God help the author who practises it on his own writings: if he does he feels condemned to rewrite endlessly every page and every book becomes an open-ended work.

# The Fear of Spiders

A very young friend of mine in the third grade was assigned a research composition on insects, and he triumphantly started it like this: 'Insects get their names from having six legs.' The teacher pointed out to him that the name would have been correct if the legs had been seven, and he said that the difference between six and seven is small.

The difference between six and eight must be enormously larger. Many people, children and adults, men and women, brave and fearful, are deeply repelled by spiders, and if they are asked why spiders in particular, they usually answer: 'Because they have eight legs.'

I am not proud to confess that I am among them and am unable to forget one of my most anguishing nights: I must have been nine and was sleeping in the country in a room in which the wallpaper had come unglued from the wall and amplified the noises like a drum. I was about to fall asleep and had perceived a ticking sound. I turned on the light and there was the monster: black, all legs, it was descending towards the night table with the uncertain and inexorable step of Death. I called for help, and the maid squashed the apparition (an innoculous Tegenaria) with obvious satisfaction. This distant terror of spiders lulled by now by the disappearance of these adversaries from the urban environment in which I live has been brought to mind when reading an article published a few weeks ago in *La Stampa*, in which Isabella Lattes Coifman describes certain discoveries concerning the sexual life of spiders. All of them, from the minuscule scarlet spiders which live in the porosity of rocks to the obese, crossbearing spiders stationed head-on at the centre of their geometric webs, inflict on me a revulsion-horror which is totally unjustified and highly specific. I would touch a toad, a worm, a mouse, a cockroach, a snail if I were insured against possible harm, even a scorpion or a cobra – a spider never. Why?

The answer I have recorded above is classic, but it is a non-answer. It is obvious that there is no reason whatsoever for eight legs to be more repulsive than six or four, even if one admits that we, the spiders' enemies, before giving in to the ritual shudder, take the time to count its legs: which for all that are often seven or even less, because spiders are subject to accidents (on the road or at work) four times more than we bipeds, and because, if seized by a leg, get rid of it easily without great concern: 'they know' that a new one will grow during the next moulting. But neither do the other usual answers satisfy.

There are those who say that they hate spiders because they are cruel. They are, but no more than other animals. Whoever has seen a cat play for hours with a mutilated and moribund mouse will at the most feel pity for the mouse; as for the cat, it has our understanding, and perhaps an iniquitous mammal solidarity although its cruelty is (at least in appearance) more gratuitous and more responsible than that of the spider. The animal cannot be the object of moral judgements ('because all your grace/is the fruit of nature'); and even less should we be tempted to export our human moral standards to animals as far from us as the Arthropoda. Judging from the behaviour of wounded or amputated spiders and insects it is improbable that they experience anything analogous to our pain, and it is instead probable that our compassion for the spider's victim is wasted: it would be better to direct it, for example, to battery raised chickens, or to man's human victims.

Some people hate spiders because they are 'ugly and hairy'. Some in fact are hairy, but then if hair were repulsive to us, why do we touch with pleasure so many other animals covered with hair? Actually we love precisely their hair, with a strange love that leads us to clip them, or even skin them, and even adorn ourselves with their fur. Nor do other fuzzy little insects such as bees and bumble bees inspire revulsion. As for ugliness, there does not exist a more ambiguous and debated term: it would be wise to confine its use to man's works. There are no ugly natural objects, nor animals, plants, stones or waters, and even less are there ugly stars in the sky. We have been taught to call ugly ('ugly beast') certain animals considered harmful, but their natural ugliness ends there.

Do we hate spiders because they lay in ambush? I believe that this too is moralistic. If anything, the spider's web should be admired; and indeed it is by all those who are immune to our phobia or have overcome it. To watch the birth of a nest of little spiders, who as soon as they have come out of the egg scurry about on a hedge and each gets busy weaving its web is not a horrible but a marvellous spectacle. Each of them is as big as the head of a pin· but is born a master: without *pentimenti*, without mistakes, it weaves its web the size of a commemorative stamp and sets itself to wait for the minuscule prey. It is born an adult, its wisdom has been transmitted to it together with its shape. It does not have to go to school: is this what horrifies us?

There are bolder explanations. After all, who can stop a psychologist of the unconscious in the exercise of his function? They have fired all their big guns at the spiders. Their hairiness is supposed to have a sexual significance, and the repulsion we feel supposedly reveals our unconscious rejection of sex: this is how we express it and at the same time this is how we try to free ourselves of it.

The capturing technique of the spider who covers with filaments the prey caught in the web supposedly turns it into a maternal symbol: the spider is the enemy-mother who envelops and encompasses, who wants to make us re-enter the womb from which we have issued, bind us tightly to take us back to the impotence of infancy, subject us again to her power; and there are those who remember that in almost all languages the spider's name is feminine, that the larger and more beautiful webs are those of the female spiders, and that some females devour the male after or during mating. This last fact is strange and horrendous when seen from our human observatory; but it is unclear how an aversion can be born from an observation that almost no one has made with his own eyes and that few have learned from books.

I believe that simpler explanations are preferable. In Mediterranean countries spiders are thought to be poisonous and in both Spain and Southern Italy the memory of tarantism is still alive. It was believed that the person stung by a tarantula or wolf-spider caught a fatal disease from which he could only be healed by dancing frenetically. It is proven today that the tarantula is innocuous, as are almost all spiders in our country; but there is not a child, especially in the country, whose mother does not say: 'Don't touch it, it's a spider, it's poisonous'; and childhood memories are indelible.

Perhaps there is also something else. The old cobwebs in cellars and attics are heavy with symbolic significance: they are the banners of desertion, absence, decay and oblivion. They veil human works, envelop them as though in a shroud, dead as the hands which through years and centuries built them. And one cannot ignore the furtive way, which indeed is highly specific, that spiders come on to the scene: not with the belligerent hum of wasps, not with the lightning-like determination of mice, but through invisible fissures with the slow, soundless step of ghosts: at times they lower themselves vertically from the dark ceiling within the cone of a lamp's light, unexpected, hanging from their metaphysical thread. And spectral also are their nocturnal webs, which we do not see but feel viscous on our face when in the morning we walk between the hedges along a path that nobody has yet gone down.

As for my personal and slight phobia, it has a birth certificate. It is the etching by Gustave Doré which illustrates Arachne in the twelfth canto of Dante's *Purgatory*, and with which I collided as a child. The young girl who dared challenge Minerva in the art of weaving is punished by a foul transfiguration: in the drawing she is 'almost half a spider', and is brilliantly depicted as utterly frantic, with full breasts where one would expect to see her back and from her back have sprouted six legs, knotty, hairy, painful: six legs which, together with human arms that writhe desperately, add up to eight. On his knees, before the new monster, Dante seems to be contemplating its crotches, half disgusted, half voyeur.

# Novels Dictated by Crickets

In an elegant essay written about forty years ago, Aldous Huxley, in answer to a young man who intended to become a writer and had turned to him for advice, recommended that he buy a pair of cats, observe them and describe them. He told him, if I am not mistaken, that animals, and mammals in particular, and even more particularly domestic animals, are like us, but 'with the lid off'. Their behaviour is similar to what ours would be if we lacked inhibitions. So observing them is valuable for the novelist who sets out to plumb his characters' profound motivations.

Perhaps things are not that simple. Since then ethology has been born and has rapidly matured and taught us that animals are different from each other and from us, that each animal species follows its own laws and that these laws, so far as we can succeed in understanding them, are in perfect agreement with the theories of evolution, that is, favour the conservation of the species, even if not always that of the individual. Ethologists and Pavlovians have sternly admonished us not to attribute human mental mechanisms to animals, nor describe them in anthropomorphic language. They have generally been heeded, and indeed the opposite tendency has prevailed, the tendency, that is, to describe man in zoological terms, and at all costs find the animal in man (as Desmond Morris did a trifle superficially in *The Naked Ape*); I believe that not all human actions can be interpreted in this way and that the method does not take us very far. Socrates, Newton, Bach and Leopardi were not naked apes.

Having said this, I must add that Huxley erred in his explanation, but was triumphantly right in giving that advice to his disciple. There is more: anyone who looks a bit more closely at his most famous works cannot help but notice that he must have been an attentive and gifted observer of animals in whose behaviour he had trained himself to recognise hypostases and symbols of man's virtues, vices and passions. Certainly he must have been helped along this path by the closeness of his brother Julian, the famous biologist and inspired populariser. If I were able to, I would follow Huxley's recommendation with enthusiasm and fill my house with all sorts of animals. I would make an effort not only to observe them, but also to enter into communication with them. I would not do this for a scientific purpose (for this I have neither the education nor the background), but out of affection, and because I am certain that from it I would derive an extraordinary spiritual enrichment and a more complete vision of the world. For lack of better, I read with ever renewed enjoyment and amazement many books, old and new, that talk about animals, and I feel that I draw from them a vital nourishment, independent of their literary or scientific value. They may even be full of lies, like old Pliny: it doesn't matter, their value lies in the suggestions they offer.

It is an ancient observation, ancient already at the time of Aesop (who must have known a lot about animals), that all extremes are found in animals. There are enormous and tiny animals, extremely strong and extremely weak, bold and skittish, fast and slow, cunning and foolish, splendid and horrendous: the writer has only to choose, he does not have to take into account the truths of the scientist, it is enough for him to scoop up with both hands examples from this universe of metaphors. Precisely by coming out of the human island he will find every human quality multiplied a hundred-fold, a vast thicket of prefabricated hyperbole.

Of these many are weary, worn out by use in all languages: the much-too-well-known qualities of the lion, wolf, and bull are no longer usable. But the discoveries of modern naturalists, dense and marvellous during these last years, have opened for writers a vein of ideas whose exploitation is only at its timid beginnings. In the reports of the magazines *Nature* and *Scientific American* and in the books of Konrad Lorenz and his disciples cluster the seeds of a new kind of writing, still to be discovered, which awaits its demiurge.

We have all listened, during the summer nights, to the duets of crickets. They are of many species and each sings with a rhythm and note of its own: the male calls and the female, at a distance even of two hundred metres and totally invisible, answers in tune. The duet, patient and chaste, continues for hours and gradually the two partners slowly come closer, until they make contact and mate. But it is indispensable for the female to answer correctly: an answer out of tune, even by one fourth of a tone, interrupts the dialogue, and the male goes in search of another companion, more in conformity with his innate model. It seems that this condition of exact acoustic syntony is a guarantee against the cross-breedings of different species, which would be sterile and therefore useless for the 'you must multiply' aim. It is thought that the same aim is served by the complicated courting rituals, either graceful or grotesque, observed among animals extremely different from each other, such as spiders, fishes and birds (and here one notices that the ethologists themselves are compelled to introduce into their language the term 'courtship' which is a human metaphor).

Now, a talented experimenter has observed that it is possible to alter the tonality of the cricket's song to a known and reproducable degree: its frequency (and the tone of the note emitted) depends to a very clear degree on the temperature of the environment.

It is obvious that under natural conditions both male and female are at the same temperature but if the body heat of the female (or male) is increased only by two or three degrees, its song goes one semitone higher, and the partner no longer answers: he no longer recognises in her (or in him) a possible sexual mate. From a minuscule environmental cause an incompatibility is born. Don't we have the germ of a novel here?

Spiders, especially, are an inexhaustible source of astonishment, meditation, stimuli and shivers. They are (not all of them) methodical and fanatically conservative geometrists: the common garden spider, the diadem spider, for tens of millions of years has been building his radiated web, symmetrical and in conformity with a rigid pattern. He cannot endure imperfections: if the web is damaged, he does not repair it. He destroys it and weaves a new one. During the course of research into drugs a biologist administered a small dose of LSD to a spider. The drugged spider did not remain idle, and according to the habits of his species immediately began to construct his web, but he wove a monstrous web, crooked, deformed, like the visions of drugged humans: dense and tangled in some parts, interrupted by gaps in others. His work completed, the delirious spider crouched in a corner of his web, lying in wait for an improbable prey.

It is known that many female spiders devour the male immediately or even during the sexual act: this is what at any rate praying mantises do too and bees massacre with ferocity all the drones of the hive after one of them takes off on the nuptial flight with the future queen. These are all themes full of dark significance which awaken sombre resonances in the depths of our minds as civilised men.

Uxoricide among spiders is rather normal. The female is generally larger and stronger than the male, and as soon as fecundation has taken place she tends to behave with him as with any other prey. Not always do the males put up a defence or attempt flight: in various species, one would say that they consent to nature's cynical evolutionary design, according to which, once the task of reproduction is fulfilled, their reason for being ceases and therefore also the instinct of survival is extinguished in them. But instead when male spiders put up a defence, we enter a dramatic, frenetic world which finds its human counterpart only in the criminal and psychopathic fringes of our society; or it cannot find any counterpart but invites its invention, imagining situations never dreamed of even by our writers of tragedy.

There are spiders who begin courtship by offering the female a gift: a living prey, or a prey which is alive but paralysed by venom and gagged and tied by a sheath of threads. This is not a disinterested gift. The female accepts it, eats her fill while the male waits, and afterwards she will no longer be hungry and the mating will not end in murder. Other males, dancing around the female in a courting ritual, enmesh her gradually in a tangle of thick threads and fecundate her only when the violent mate, ambivalently desired and feared, is reduced to immobility. Still others (and here who can resist the temptation of a perhaps abusive and baroque human interpretation?) behave with incredible farsightedness and foul duplicity.

In the season when the eggs open, they go on raids for females that are immature and therefore still weak and each male kidnaps and sequesters one of them. He ties her with the portentous thread fit for a thousand uses, keeps her imprisoned, feeding her meagerly (so that she won't get too strong) and defending her from possible attackers until she is sexually mature: then he fecundates and abandons her. When she has reached the peak of her full strength, the female has no difficulty in liberating herself from her bonds. We are at the uncertain borderline between crime news and comic opera. It is difficult to avoid remembering the ambiguous and stereotyped relationship between guardian and ward, between the scheming and imprisoning Don Bartolo swollen with belated lusts and the delicious Rosina kept under lock and key but a future 'viper': 'both were fit to be tied.'

Many animals, with the most varied structures, flaunt vivacious colours while the taste of their flesh is revolting, or they are poisonous: for example, goldfish and ladybirds, or, respectively, wasps and certain snakes. The gaudy colours serve as a signal and warning so that predators recognise them from afar and, taught by previous experience, refrain from attacking them. Does there exist a parallel human behaviour? In general a harmful man tends to confuse himself with the majority in order to escape identification; but he does not do so when he is, or feels he is, above the law.

One should give a little more thought to the appearance of bravoes, such as Manzoni describes them; to the use (widespread until 1900) of aggressively coloured military uniforms; and to certain characteristic forms of dress and expression which facilitate the identification of those who belong to particular groups of criminals (Apaches, members of the Mafia). Even aside from these examples I would like to invent and describe a ladybird character, seen perhaps in certain of Gogol's pages: hypochondriac, dissatisfied with himself, his fellow man and the world, irksome and full of complaints, who wears a livery recognisable from a distance (or a mannerism, or a speech defect) so that his fellow man, whom he detests, quickly becomes aware of his presence and gets out of his way.

# Domum Servavit

The 'channel' is among the most felicitous images drawn from everyday speech to satisfy the ever new needs of specialised languages. Everyone knows what a channel is: it forces water to flow from a source to an outlet between two basically insuperable banks, but the term lends itself well to describing other flowing phenomena in which 'something' (a fluid, a swarm of particles, the traffic of a highway, a human crowd, but also a sum of money, a packet of energy, information) moves in a single dimension and direction confined by material or symbolic banks. In this sense there is no doubt that a highway is a channel, as is also a telephonic communication: less to the point one speaks of television channels, because in this case the origin is one source but the outlets (the television screens) are in the millions. A TV channel is therefore a finely ramified channel, a channel only in the sense that the programme broadcast flows exclusively in the direction of the receivers set up to accept it without overflowing into other receivers.

The postal 'channel' deserves a special discussion. From its very origins (in China, perhaps six thousand years ago) it was considered essential for the message to flow between good banks, that is, that the information reach the addressee without being intercepted by strangers. To ensure the impermeability of the postal channel various and well-known artifices were excogitated, such as invisible inks and cryptographic codes, and others even more imaginative, such as writing the message on the previously shaved skull of the messenger, waiting for the hair to grow back and then sending him off; the recipient shaved the hair and read the message. However, the most practical way to guarantee secrecy is still represented by the seal and its modern equivalents. The problem of formulating a material suited to act as a seal is simple: it must receive a clear imprint, solidify rapidly, maintain the imprint within a good range of temperature, and not be too fragile. As one can see, we have here the subject of plastics and in fact the classic material of the seals of all times is the dean of plastic materials – sealing wax. Wax has little or nothing to do with its composition: its basic component is shellac, an illustrious and strange material which is worth talking about.

Shellac is the fruit of the encounter of two inventive imaginations, the extremely slow imagination of evolution or nature, which created it, and the swift and flexible imagination of man, which has found it suitable for various uses. The true inventor of shellac is an insect of lowly habits: its curriculum, linear and bare, is a parody of the guaranteed utopia about which there is so much talk today. Males and females of the creature in question begin their career in the guise of reddish larvae, barely visible to the naked eye; in innumerable swarms they lazily explore the small branches of certain exotic trees until they find a crack in the bark which allows them to insert their proboscis until it penetrates the succulent wood: at this point they are settled and insured, they will have no more problems for the rest of their lives, but neither will they have experiences, emotions, sensations. They are infinite in number, millions of individuals on a single tree, and in fact the term lacquer with which the product they secrete is designated in all languages derives from an ancient Sanskrit word which means 'one hundred thousand'.

The hundred thousand tiny parasites pump lymph and swell in silence, but even creatures with the best of guarantees must nevertheless develop an art to protect their rears. Their art is a chemical art worthy of great respect: they transform the vegetal juice into a resin whose properties are neither banal nor lowly, in fact shellac. They exude it from their pores, covering not only their rears but their entire body; they're so densely packed that the covering of one individual ends by fusing and welding with that of its neighbours, so that the infested branches are covered by a compact and shiny crust which must have attracted man's attention since ancient times. Beneath this crust lies the army of suckers, protected and imprisoned. The males communicate with the outside only through a small hole which allows them to breathe; the females also keep open a second small hole, the extension of their genital orifice through which fecundation will take place. After a few weeks sexual maturity is attained, and at this point destinies diverge. The female continues not to move, actually loses her legs since they are no longer any use to her. Like the exemplary matron of antiquity, *domum servavit, lanum fecit*: she stayed at home, spinning wool, in our case exuding resin. The male braces himself for a fleeting initiative: having reached maturity, he comes out of jail and fecundates several females without direct contact but utilising the hole predisposed for this purpose; and then he dies. The fecundated females, and practically all of them are, do not leave their cell and continue to secrete resin: inside the cell they deposit their eggs, survive until they open, then they too die and larvae come out of the eggs and commence a new cycle. To try to extract a human moral from the animals around us is an ancient and illogical vice; to indulge in it is risky but amusing. One is tempted to say with Aesop: 'the fable teaches' that the price for guaranteed abundance can be high, and early retirement can be deadly.

Shellac is a noble resin; it is transparent, withstands impact and sunlight, has a pleasant odour, is glossy, and what's more has another curious and unique virtue, certainly useful to its insect inventor: when exposed to humidity its permeability to water diminishes instead of increasing, as does that of almost all other organic materials; in short it behaves on the molecular scale like an umbrella that opens spontaneously at the beginning of a downpour.

The human discoverer of shellac is unknown: he must have
been one of the thousand unknown Darwins and Newtons
who have constellated all past eras and constellate ours, and
who expend their talent in a society that does not understand
them, yoked to repetitive and boring work. Someone in short
who must have noticed that the protective properties of shellac
were adapted to protecting something else besides the slothful
and gluttonous parasite that secretes it. They could especially
be used to protect the secrecy of the mails, that is, plug the
leaks in the channel travelled by written messages, because
that is what seals have done since the most ancient times; but
resin also has other uses. Since equally ancient times it was
melted, mixed with pigments of various colours, then left to
solidify in small blocks. These were pressed forcefully against
wooden pieces being turned on the lathe: the heat of the
attrition again melted the coloured shellac which was uni-
formly distributed on the wood 'with the thickness of a man's
fingernail', brightening its appearance and protecting it from
dampness. This singular method of varnishing was still in use
in India at the beginning of the century and Kipling described
it.

Today shellac is employed mainly as a bonding agent in
spirit-based varnishes. It is clear that with the system described
above one can cover only pieces that have cylindrical symmetry
and dimensions for the lathe. For use as a varnish it was
necessary to find a solvent apt to melt the resin and the
technology to reduce it to an easily soluble form. The solvent
was found towards the beginning of the 1800s and it is our
common rectified alcohol: the technology, today obsolete,
was astonishing.

The resin was melted and filtered through canvas to eliminate insects and fragments of wood. It was left to harden in the
shape of flat blocks weighing from five to six kilos, which
were then heated again so that the resin would become creamy.
At this point there appeared on the stage the 'spreaders', who
for the most part were very young women: from sunrise to

sunset they squatted on the ground, seized a block at five places with their hands, their teeth, and the toes of their feet, and then straightened out, quickly opening their arms: the block was thus spread out in a sheet with a pentagonal contour as tall as the spreader, transparent and fragile as glass, which was then shattered into thin and therefore easily soluble scales. With this gesture, repeated an infinite number of times, the little girl-machines rose from the closed position of a germ to the open one of the flower. It must have been a comical ballet, cruel and gentle: in it one sees an ingenuity as cynical as that which deprived the female insects of their legs; an ingenuity which did not hesitate to make a tool of man, regress him to an animalesque act in which the mouth, the word workshop, once again became an instrument for biting.

# On Obscure Writing

One should never impose limits or rules on creative writing. Those who do, generally obey political taboos or atavistic fears: actually, a written text no matter how it is written, is less dangerous than is commonly thought; the famous judgment passed on Silvio Pellico's *My Prisons*, which supposedly harmed Austria 'more than a lost battle', is hyperbolic. It is a matter of practical observation that a book or a story, whether its intentions be good or bad, are essentially inert and innocuous objects; also in their most ignoble incarnations (for example, the Nazi-tinged sex and pathologic-pornographic hybrids) can only cause scant harm, certainly inferior to that produced by alcohol, smoking or corporate stress. Their intrinsic weakness is aggravated by the fact that today all writing is smothered in a few months by the mob of other writings which push up behind it. Furthermore, rules and limitations, being determined historically, tend to change often: the history of all literatures is full of episodes in which rich and valid works were opposed in the name of principles which later proved to be much more ephemeral than the works themselves; from it one can deduce that many precious books must have disappeared without leaving a trace, having been defeated in the never-ending struggle between those who write and those who prescribe how one should write. From the heights of our permissive epoch the trials (real trials in court) of Flaubert, Baudelaire, and D. H. Lawrence, seem as grotesque and ironic as the trial against Galileo, so wide does the gap

between judges and judged appear today: the former bound to
their time, the latter alive for all foreseeable futures. In short,
to legislate for the narrator is to say the least, useless. This
said, and therefore emphatically renouncing any regulative,
prohibitive or punitive claim, I would like to add that in my
opinion one should not write in an obscure manner, because a
piece of writing has all the more value and all the more hope
of diffusion and permanence, the better it is understood and
the less it lends itself to equivocal interpretations.

It is obvious that perfectly lucid writing presupposes a
totally conscious writer, and this does not correspond to
reality. We are made up of ego and id, spirit and flesh, and
furthermore nucleic acids, traditions, hormones, remote and
recent experiences and traumas; therefore we are condemned
to carry from crib to grave, a *Doppelganger*, a mute and
faceless brother who nevertheless is co-responsible for our
actions, and so for all of our pages. It is known that no author
deeply understands what he has written and all authors have
had the opportunity of being astonished by the beautiful and
awful things that the critics have found in their works and that
they did not know they had put there; many books contain
plagiarisms, conceptual or verbal, of which the authors declare
in good faith they were unaware. This is a fact one cannot
fight against: this source of unknowability and irrationality
which each of us harbours must be accepted, even authorised
to express itself in its (necessarily obscure) language, but
should not be considered the best or only source of expression.
It is not true that the only authentic writing is that which
'comes from the heart', and which actually comes from all the
distinct ingredients of consciousness mentioned above. This
time-honoured opinion is based on the presupposition that the
heart which 'dictates inside' is an organ different from that of
reason and more noble, and that the language of the heart is
the same for everyone, which it is not. Far from being universal
in time and space, the language of the heart is capricious,
contaminated, and as unstable as fashion, of which it is indeed

a part: nor can one firmly maintain that it is the same within the confines of a country and an epoch. To put it differently, it isn't a language at all, or at the most a vernacular, an argot, if not an individual invention.

So he who writes the language of the heart can turn out to be indecipherable, and it is then right to ask oneself what was the purpose of his writing: in fact (I would say that this is a widely acceptable postulate) writing serves to communicate, transmit information or feelings from mind to mind, from place to place and from time to time. And he who is not understood by anyone does not transmit anything, he cries in the desert. When this happens the well-intentioned reader must be reassured: if he does not understand the text it is the author's fault, not his. It is up to the writer to make himself understood by those who wish to understand him: it is his trade, writing is a public service and the willing reader must not be disappointed.

As for this reader – and I have the strange impression of having him alongside me as I write – I must admit that I have slightly idealised him. He is similar to the perfect gases of thermo-dynamics, perfect only inasmuch as their behaviour is perfectly foreseeable on the basis of simple laws, whereas real gases are more complicated. My 'perfect' reader is not a scholar but neither is he an ignoramus; he does not read because he has to, nor as a pastime, nor to make a splash in society, but because he is curious about many things, wishes to choose among them and does not wish to delegate this choice to anyone; he knows the limits of his competence and education, and directs his choices accordingly; in the present case he has with good will chosen my books and would experience irritation or pain if he did not understand line by line what I had written, indeed, have written for him: in fact I write *for him* and not for the critics, nor for the powerful of the Earth, nor for myself. If he did not understand me, he would feel unjustly humiliated, and I would be guilty of a breach of contract.

Here it is necessary to confront an objection: sometimes one writes (or speaks) not to communicate but to give vent to tension, or joy, or pain, and then one also cries in the desert, moans, laughs, sings, and howls.

For those who howl, provided they have valid reasons for doing so, one must have understanding: weeping and mourning whether restrained or theatrical, are beneficial because they alleviate pain. Jacob howls over Joseph's bloodied coat; in many civilisations the howled mourning is ritual and prescribed. But then the howl is an extreme recourse, good for the individual as tears, inert and uncouth if understood as a language, because that by definition it is not: the inarticulate is not articulate, noise is not sound. For this reason I am fed up with the praises of texts which (I quote at random) 'sound at the limit of the ineffable, the non-existent, the whine of an animal'. I'm tired of 'dense magmatic imposters', of 'semantic refusals', and stale innovations. White pages are white, and it is best to call them white; if the king is naked, it is honest to say that he is naked.

Personally I am also tired of the praise lavished in life and death on Ezra Pound, who was perhaps even a great poet, but in order to make sure he would not be understood even wrote in Chinese at times, and I am convinced that his poetic obscurity had the same root as his belief in the superman, which led him first to Fascism and then to self-alienation: both germinated from his contempt for the reader. Perhaps the American court which judged Pound mentally ill was right: a writer by instinct, he must have been an abominable thinker and that is confirmed by his political behaviour and his maniacal hatred of bankers. Now whoever does not know how to reason must be cured, and within the limits of possibility respected, even if, like Ezra Pound, he lends himself to making Nazi propaganda against his own country at war with Hitler's Germany: but he must not be praised, nor held up as an example, because it is better to be sane than insane. The effable is preferable to the ineffable, the human word to the animal whine.

It is not by chance that the two least decipherable German poets, Trakl and Celan, both died as suicides, separated by two generations. Their common destiny makes one think about the obscurity of their poetry as a pre-killing, a not-wanting-to-be, a flight from the world of which the intentional death was the crown. They must be respected because their 'animal whine' was dreadfully motivated: for Trakl, by the wreckage of the Habsburg empire, in which he believed, in the maelstrom of the First World War; for Celan, a German Jew, who by a miracle survived the German slaughter, by the uprooting and unappeasable anguish in the face of triumphant Death. For Celan, above all, because he is our contemporary (1920–1970), we must speak with more seriousness and greater responsibility.

It is evident that his song is tragic and noble, but confusedly so: to penetrate it is a desperate enterprise for the common reader but also for the critic. Celan's obscurity is neither contempt for the reader nor expressive inadequacy, nor lazy abandonment to the flow of the unconscious: it truly is a reflection of the obscurity of his fate and his generation, and it grows ever denser around the reader, gripping him as in an ice-cold iron vice, from the raw lucidity of *Death Flight* (1945) to the atrocious chaos without a glimmer of light of his last compositions. This darkness grows from page to page until the last inarticulate babble consternates like the rattle of a dying man, and in fact that is just what it is. It attracts us as chasms attract us, but at the same time it also defrauds us of something that should have been said and was not, and so it frustrates and turns us away. I believe that Celan the poet should be meditated upon and pitied rather than imitated. If his is a message, it gets lost in the 'background noise': it is not a communication, it is not a language, or at most it is a dark and truncated language precisely like that of a person who is about to die and is alone, as we all will be at the point of death. But since we the living are not alone, we must not write as if we were alone. As long as we live we have a responsibility:

we must answer for what we write, word by word, and make sure that every word reaches its target.

For the rest, talking to one's fellow man in a language that he cannot understand may be the bad habit of some revolutionaries, but it is not at all a revolutionary instrument: it is on the contrary, an ancient repressive artifice, known to all churches, the typical vice of our political class, the foundation of all colonial empires. It is a subtle way of imposing one's rank: when Fra Cristoforo (in Manzoni's *The Betrothed*) says, '*Omnia munda mundis*' in Latin to Fra Fazio, who has no Latin, the latter 'at hearing those words pregnant with a mysterious meaning, and pronounced so resolutely ... it seemed that in them must be contained the solution to all his doubts. He calmed down, and said "Enough! You know more than I do."'

Nor is it true that one can express only through verbal obscurity that other obscurity of which we are the children, and which lies in our depths. It is not true that disorder is necessary to depict disorder; it is not true that the chaos of the written page is the best symbol of the ultimate chaos to which we are fated: to believe this is a typical vice of our uncertain century. As long as we live, and whatever fate may have been assigned to us, or we have chosen, there is no doubt that the better the quality of our communication, the more useful (and agreeable) to ourselves and others we will be and the longer we will be remembered. He who does not know how to communicate, or communicates badly, in a code that belongs only to him or a few others, is unhappy, and spreads unhappiness around him. If he communicates badly deliberately, he is wicked or at least a discourteous person, because he imposes labour, anguish, or boredom on his readers.

Understandably, for the message to be valid, clarity is a necessary but not sufficient condition: one can be clear and boring, clear and useless, clear and untruthful, clear and vulgar, but these are subjects for another discussion. If one is not clear there is no message at all, the animal whine is acceptable coming from animals, from the dying, the mad and the desperate: the healthy and whole man who adopts it is a hypocrite or a fool, and condemns himself to not having any readers. Discourse among men in the tongue of men is preferable to the animal whine, and it is hard to see why it should be less poetic than in the whine.

But, I repeat, these are preferences of mine, not standards. Whoever writes is free to choose the language or non-language that suits him best, and everything is possible: writing which is obscure for its own author may be luminous and open for him who reads; and the writing not understood by its contemporaries may become clear and illustrious decades and centuries later.

# The Children's International

Some time ago I happened to observe a small group of children who were playing hopscotch in a Ukrainian village. I could not understand what they were saying to each other, much less what they called their game (which in Italy is called 'Bell', 'Week', and 'World'). But from all appearances the rules they followed were the same as ours. The game consists in tracing on the ground a schematic design of boxes and then negotiating it according to various successive rules: with closed eyes and without treading on the lines; with open eyes but hopping only on one foot and picking up a small stone in the boxes; balancing another stone on the head, the back of the hand, a foot, etc.; whoever makes a mistake must give up his turn to another player and whoever completes the entire programme in the shortest time wins.

At that time the pattern of the boxes was the same in the Ukraine and Italy; today it is slightly changed here. It would be interesting to go and see if it has been changed in the same way in the Ukraine, a good probability, because the universe of children's games is unified by mysterious channels.

An English married couple have devoted themselves to the study of these channels with philological diligence, and have suffused their study with that precious combination of rigour and imagination which distinguishes British civilisation. Iona and Peter Opie have spent the decade from 1959 to 1969 interviewing more than ten thousand children: they asked them only to describe the rules of their spontaneous games, those in which adults have never intruded, and for which no equipment is needed, not even a ball or a bat – 'All you need is players.'

Besides these interviews they have consulted an enormous mass of documentary material, drawing from other studies performed in distant countries, and also from old and recent literary testimony. From this was born a book full of surprises, *Children's Games in Street and Playground*,* which should be followed by another book on games in which a ball, billiard balls, or other equipment is necessary.

Like every good book, this too answers certain questions yet gives rise to many more numerous and stimulating ones. The games here described, although observed in all of Europe and also outside it, are familiar to every Italian who has or had children, or has contact with children, or even only preserves some memories of his own childhood. Obviously with different names but with strangely similar rituals we find in their many variations of playing 'Catching opponents', 'hiding', 'prisoners' base', and 'cops and robbers', and up to this point there is nothing very strange; these games are rational: they reproduce the situations and emotions in the hunt and ambush and it is probable that their roots lie deep in our heredity as hunting, social and contentious mammals. Also the young of dogs and cats although they belong to races domesticated for thousands of years, reproduce in their play the rituals of hunt and struggle.

On the other hand, it is difficult to understand why abstract games or rituals, apparently devoid of utilitarian significance, are found almost exactly identical in countries very far from each other. An example is the well-known game of 'four corners', which is not rational. There is no reason why the four players who occupy the corners should not remain in their places indefinitely, so that the child saddled with the disagreeable role of being 'it' should remain 'it' to the bitter

* *Oxford University Press*, 1969.

end. And yet, down the centuries (the game is recorded since 1600), and in a good part of the world, the ritual is the same as if, instead of a game, a religious ceremony were at stake.

The same can be said of the graceful but (for an adult) irritating game which in Italy is called 'queen, little queen'. For anyone who does not remember, the 'little queen' is placed at one end of the field, and in front of her (or him), lined up at a distance of twenty metres, stand the other players. Each of these in turn ask the queen how many steps must be taken to arrive at 'her castle', and the queen answers in the most capricious way but in accordance with a traditional lexicon, that the steps are, for instance, four giant steps or six lion steps or four ant steps, or even ten shrimp steps; in this last case, the player-victim is obliged to go backwards.

As can be seen, the game could not be more unfair*; we have here in substance a childish and abstemious version of 'Passatella' (pass the wine jug) for always and only the child whom the queen has decided to favour wins, that is, reaches the castle; having become queen in turn, the child will return the favour to the previous queen, in keeping with disagreeable Mafia protocol etiquette. No space is left for initiative, intelligence and ability on the part of the players; despite all this, the game is played in many countries and the variations are few (but singular: in the British Isles the Opies have recorded among others also the caterpillar step, the banana-peel step, and the watering-can step; the latter consists in spitting as far as one can and stopping where the spit landed).

Almost all 'catch' games provide for a sanctuary (given different names: among us it is 'the touch') in which the pursued is safe from capture; very popular is the variation which in Italy is called 'high up' and forty years ago 'porter's lodge', which in France is 'le chat-perché' (the perching cat) and in England 'off-ground-he': incidentally, 'he' or 'it' is the

---

* English in original.

player whom we Italians call 'under'. In this version safety is achieved simply by climbing on any surface that projects above ground level. 'Higher up' is known all over the world.

Equally international are the rituals which proceed the beginning of any games. In general they consist in a drawing of lots to designate the player or players who are 'under', who, that is, take over the less agreeable role in each single game, but a fair drawing, for example, the system of the shortest straw, is rarely resorted to. Widespread and fair, but cumbersome inasmuch as it allows only for choosing between two players at a time, is the so-called (in Europe) 'Chinese morra', which I expect everyone knows: in almost all countries the three signs of the hand indicate the stone, the scissors and paper, and justification as to why each sign circularly wins over the next sign is the same.

Again, in passing: I do not find recorded by the diligent Opies a kind of choosing up that I saw practised in Piedmont; the two contenders respectively declare for odd or even, but then, instead of resorting to the classical morra, one of the two pinchs the back of his left hand; the winner is the one who has foreseen the even or odd number of wrinkles formed in the skin.

The Opies have also not devoted too much attention to the shout of truce, used everywhere to ask for or impose an armistice in competitive games: they only say that in the British Isles one shouts 'Barley!' without investigating the origins of this curious term. In Italy and today, as far as I know, the shout is 'It's dead', whose meaning is obvious, and 'It's alive' to resume the game. Fifty or sixty years ago in Piedmont (I don't know if elsewhere also) the shout was *'marsa!'* I have a question for any reader who might have an appetite for this minor anthropology: *'Marsa'* in Arabic is port, hence Marsala, Marsa Matruh, and other place names; it probably also stands for 'shelter, asylum'. Could this be the origin of the signal, which thus comes from the South? To accept this it would be necessary for older people who in their childhood played hide and seek in Sicily to try to remember how 'time out' was called in their time and their town. I beg them to do so.

Despite all the quicker and more equitable systems that it is easy to imagine, and which in fact have been imagined, the most popular choosing up in the world is called 'the count', and here the story becomes interesting. I believe that everybody remembers at least one or two of the counting jingles he used or heard used as a child. They are rhythmic sing-songs, generally with four strong accents in each verse; the Opies, on the basis of other, previous collections, have recorded more than two hundred in all of Europe and in the English-speaking countries. Some of them, the more recent, are rationalised and have a more or less self-contained meaning, but it is evident that the more ancient are preferred, and these are pure abracadabra. Nevertheless, in them certain international lodes can be recognised, but not more than four or five: the rhythm and often the rhyme are preserved unchanged, while the words are distorted in keeping with the local language.

It is clear that the ritual character prevails over the utilitarian purpose of the choosing up, in which the meaning of the words is unimportant (just think of all the protests provoked by the Church's decision to do away with the Latin Mass!), while very important is the repetition of gestures and words, which, being magical, must be felt as 'sybilline'. It is therefore a matter of words reduced to pure sounds, and this explains the difficulties one encounters in searching for their origins. However, for one of the lodes mentioned above they have been found: although the 'counts' of this lode are spread throughout the former British Empire, their origin is not English but Welsh, and does not reproduce the ancient Welsh tongue which has almost disappeared today, but the series of numerals, probably pre-Celtic, which, in remote times were used by the cattle drovers in Wales only to count the heads of cattle. Apparently, they used that and not ordinary counting with an apotropoeic purpose, that is, so that the evil spirits would not understand, and would not remove any animal from the herd by stealing it and making it fall sick. It is obvious that these 'counts' owe their success precisely to their centuries-old incomprehensibility.

A similar story but more modern, has been reconstructed by an Italian scholar, Matizia Marroni Lumbroso. As a little girl in Via Reggio she had learned this 'count': *'Inimini mani mo/chissania baisto/effiala retingo/inimini mani mo'*. Many years later she found out that it was an English count: 'Eeny meeny miny mo/catch a nigger by his toe/if he hollers let him go/eeny meeny miny mo', and that it had been taught to a small group of Italian children by an English lady. The 'count' had promptly struck root, and it is quite possible that it still circulates today precisely because to Italian ears it was devoid of meaning and therefore profoundly suggestive – at any rate also in English only the second and third lines have a semblance of meaning. The rest is pure incantation.

In conclusion, not only the strange 'counts' are used everywhere, but everywhere more or less the same 'counts' are used. It would be superficial to conclude that the 'counts', and more generally all spontaneous games, are international because 'children are the same the whole world over'. Why are they? Is their play the same everywhere because it is born from a biological inheritance, because it reproduces an innate need of theirs (and ours) for a norm? Or are their games only spontaneous in appearance and in fact reproduce (by symbol or caricature) the 'games' of the adults? The fact remains that political frontiers are impervious to our verbal cultures, while the substantially non-verbal civilisation of play crosses them with the happy freedom of the wind and the clouds.

# Going Back to School

I have overcome the barriers of shyness and laziness and at the age of sixty I have registered for courses at a very serious institution where a foreign language which I know very badly is being taught. I wanted to know it better, out of pure intellectual curiosity: I had learned its elements by ear under conditions of hardship and had then used it for years because of my work, interested only in practicalities, that is, to understand and make myself understood, and neglecting its singularities, its grammar and syntax.

Entering the classroom for the first lesson was traumatic: I am an alien, a Martian; this is not my place. We were about twenty pupils, of whom only three were males; two women were visibly over thirty, all the others, men and women, were students in their twenties. The teacher, also young, was educated, pleasant, intelligent, quite adept at overcoming his students' reserve and bashfulness, expert in the art of teaching and well aware of the obstacles that hinder the flow of learning.

He began the course with a frank and honest speech. One can study a foreign language for many different purposes, and therefore it can be taught with different methods; strictly speaking, the teaching should be custom-made, moulded to the aspirations, abilities and previous knowledge of each individual pupil; since this is impossible, compromises must be made. Some wish to (or must) learn a language only to be able to read it or know it as literature, or speak it like a tourist, or transact business, or write business letters, or communicate as a technician with a colleague; but within this multitude of purposes can be traced a demarcation line between passive learning (to receive without transmitting) and active learning (to receive and transmit). Well, don't have any illusions: the more gifted among you will manage to understand passively the spoken or written language almost in its entirety; only a genius, at your age (and he obviously referred to the age of the majority), can succeed in speaking or writing it without mistakes: unless a sojourn abroad of at least six months of total immersion, that is, without hearing or pronouncing a word of Italian, is possible.

Already from the first lesson I realised how cruelly different it is to learn at twenty, forty, or sixty. I thought I had normal hearing: I do, but only for Italian. It is one thing to listen to a speech in one's own tongue where even if you miss a syllable or a word, you have no difficulty in interpolating it unconsciously, or guessing it with a rapid reasoning by exclusion. But if the language is not yours, missing a syllable is like missing the bus: the talk proceeds while you thrash about trying to reconstruct the missing link. Your comprehension can be obfuscated simply by an echo bouncing off the walls or a trolley passing in the street, but your young classmates show no sign of discomfort. Further difficulties arise because of your eyesight. I would be unfair if I complained about mine; in everyday life it bothers me a little perhaps, only in museums, where one must continually change the focus to see now close up, now from a distance. This is also what happens in school; agility in focusing is the necessity of every moment, the eye must jump innumerable times from notebook to blackboard and to the teacher's face. If you are wearing bifocals, things aren't too bad; if you're not, your left hand is involved in a fatiguing exercise of taking them on and off.

There are difficulties which are more serious because they are more profound. We know that in the process of learning there are three distinct phases: to imprint it on the memory, to hold on to it, and to recall it when required. The last two are preserved reasonably well: once the notion is imprinted, it remains so indefinitely; to recall it is not difficult, actually, as the years go by one ends by learning certain tricks so that the experience of a word or conception which one has 'on the tip of the tongue' becomes rarer. But on the other hand, to engrave it on the memory becomes ever more difficult. One must 'learn to learn': it is no longer enough to let the notion reach storage and be deposited there on its own. It won't stay there, or not for long: it enters and immediately leaves, volatilises, leaving behind only irritating, blurred traces. One must learn to intervene forcibly, wedge it into its niche as if with a hammer; it can be done, but it takes time and effort. One must take notes methodically, read them over again as many times as necessary, at a distance of weeks or months. What's more, one realises that, paradoxically, it is just as difficult to erase, that is, unlearn mistaken notions. Everything goes as if an hypothetical wax had turned harder: harder to engrave, harder to erase. Those errors of vocabulary or grammar which it is so easy to acquire by studying in a dilettante-like fashion will later demand method, patience, and a great deal of energy to be chipped away.

On the other hand, age does not bring with it only disadvantages. After all one has learned a few tricks along the way; it is easier to recognise the difference between the net and the gross, that is, between what notions should be accepted and carefully stored, what others can be examined and set aside. One has more time, more calm, and less distractions; one possesses (perhaps even without knowing) an organic body of information in which the new information inserts itself like a key in a lock. There are old curiosities which have waited for ten or twenty years to be satisfied, and the notions one longs for or desires imprint themselves better.

Above all, one's goals have changed. Also in the most fortunate cases, even after compulsory schooling (in which the motivation is generally scant) the student's motivation is only indirect. He does not study to learn, but to obtain a degree which entitles him to continue his studies, or makes it possible to earn a living; only rarely does he fully understand the correlation that ties learning to professional competence: also because, unfortunately, this correlation often does not exist. But also when he is rationally convinced of the long-term usefulness of his studies, his real and proper interest can still be weak. In contrast, the older person who decides to undertake a course of study with full freedom of choice, without constricting schedules, obligatory presences, fear of controls, exams, or even only an unfavourable judgment, experiences a feeling of lightness, of free will, which the above-described handicaps and the hard school benches cannot contaminate.

It is study, it is self-improvement and growth, and it is also play, theatre, and luxury. Play, that is, exercise as an end in itself, but regulated and orderly, is typical of the child, but in playing at going back to school one finds again the savour of childhood, delicate and forgotten. The competition with one's classmates, victorious or not, is a contact with the young on an equal footing, a fair and open contest that is impossible to realise elsewhere. The fences between the generations fall; one is forced to set aside the boring authority of older people, and is led to render homage to the superior mental resources of the young who sit next to one without derision, commiseration or contempt and become one's friends. What's more, making oneself the gift of an agreeable activity which lacks an immediate purpose is a luxury that costs little and offers much: it is like receiving, free of charge or almost, a rare and beautiful object.

# Ex-Chemist

The bond between a man and his profession is similar to that which ties him to his country; it is just as complex, often ambivalent, and in general it is understood completely only when it is broken: by exile or emigration in the case of one's country, by retirement in the case of a trade or profession. I left the trade of chemist several years ago, but only now do I feel I have the necessary detachment to see it in its entirety and understand how much it pervades me and how much I owe it.

I do not refer to the fact that during my imprisonment in Auschwitz it saved my life, nor to the reasonable livelihood I got from it for thirty years, nor to the pension to which it entitled me. Instead I would like to describe other benefits that I think I have obtained from it, and which are all related to the new trade I have gone on to, that is, the trade of writing. A need for qualification immediately arises. Writing is not really a trade, or at least in my opinion it should not be one: it is a creative activity and therefore it baulks at schedules and deadlines, commitments to customers and bosses. Nevertheless, writing is a way of 'producing', indeed a process of transformation: the writer transforms his experiences into a form that is accessible and attractive to the 'customer' who will be the reader. The experiences (in the broad sense: life experiences) are therefore raw material: the writer who lacks them works in a void, he thinks he's writing but his pages are empty. Now, the things I have seen, experienced, and done during my preceding incarnation are today for me as writer a precious source of raw materials, of events to narrate, and not only events: also of those fundamental emotions which are one's way of measuring oneself against matter (an impartial, imperturbable, but extremely harsh judge: if one makes a mistake, one is pitilessly punished) and thus of winning and losing. This last is a painful but salutary experience without which one does not become adult and responsible. I believe that every colleague of mine in chemistry can confirm this: more is learned from one's errors than from one's successes. For example: to formulate an explicative hypothesis, believe in it, grow fond of it, check it (oh, the temptation of falsifying data, of giving them a small flick of the thumb!) and in the end discover that it is mistaken – this is a cycle that in the chemist's trade is encountered only too often 'in a pure state', but can easily be recognised in innumerable other human itineraries. He who goes through it honestly issues from it matured.

There are other benefits, other gifts that the chemist offers the writer. The habit of penetrating matter, of wanting to know its composition and structure, foreseeing its properties and behaviour, leads to an insight,* a mental habit of concreteness and concision, the constant desire not to stop at the surface of things. Chemistry is the art of separating, weighing and distinguishing: these are three useful exercises also for the person who sets out to describe events or give body to his own imagination. Moreover, there is an immense patrimony of metaphors that the writer can take from the chemistry of today and yesterday which those who have not frequented the laboratory and factory know only approximately. The layman knows what to filter, crystallise, and distil means, but he knows it only at second hand: he does not know 'the passion infused by them', he does not know the emotions that are tied to these gestures, has not perceived the symbolic shadow they

* English in original.

cast. Also just on the plane of comparisons the militant chemist finds himself in possession of unsuspected wealth: 'black as ...', 'bitter as ...'; viscous, tenacious, heavy, fetid, fluid, volatile, inert, flammable: these are all qualities the chemist knows well and for each of them he knows how to choose a substance which contains it to a prominent and exemplary degree. I, an ex-chemist, by now atrophied and ill-equipped if I were to go back to a laboratory, am almost ashamed when in my writing I derive profit from this repertory: I feel I am enjoying an illicit advantage *vis-à-vis* my new writer col- leagues who do not have a militancy like mine behind them.

For all these reasons, when a reader expresses amazement at the fact that I a chemist have chosen the road of the writer, I feel authorised to answer that I write precisely because I am a chemist: my old trade has been largely transfused into my new one.

# Signs on Stone

'*Adhaesit pavimento anima mea*', my soul clings to the pavement: thus Psalm 119 which Dante quotes in *Purgatory*, and which, however, is translated in different ways. It adhered to the pavement for varied reasons and for a brief time, and this contact has not been completely useless; it was somewhat akin to an exploration. Pavements are a very civilised institution; it is known by today's Romans who do not have them and when they walk on foot must squeeze through unnerving labyrinths between cars parked too close to the walls. It was known to the ancient Romans who on the contrary had built them well above the ground at Pompeii; it was also known to Fra Cristoforo in Manzoni's nóvel *The Betrothed* who in fact became a monk because a particular pavement was not there, or was muddy, or too narrow, so that he had been forced into a nasty encounter that made him change his name and destiny.

The pavements of my city (and, I have no doubt, those of any other city) are full of surprisés. The most recent ones are made of asphalt, and this is madness: the further we progress on the road of austerity the more it seems stupid to use organic compounds to walk on. Perhaps the time is not far away when urban asphalt will be re-exhumed with the caution used to detach frescoes; it will be collected, classified, hydrogenated, redistilled to extract from it the noble fractions it potentially contains. Or perhaps the pavements made of asphalt will be buried under new layers of some other new-fangled

material, it is hoped less prodigal, and then future archaeologists will find set in it, like Pliocene insects in amber,
Coca Cola caps and the rip-off tabs from beer cans, drawing
from them data on the quality and quantity of our alimentary
choices. Thus will be repeated the phenomenon which to our
eyes has rendered interesting and noble the *Kokkenmoddingen*,
those small hills composed exclusively of mollusc shells, fish
and seagull bones, which today's archaeologists unearth on the
coasts of Denmark; they were mounds of refuse which slowly
grew, beginning approximately seven thousand years ago
around the poor fishing villages, and are no illustrious fossils.

Older and more typical pavements are instead made of slabs
of hard stone patiently shaped and chiselled by hand. Their
degree of erosion permits a rough dating: the more ancient
slabs are smooth and polished, furbished by the steps of
generations of pedestrians, and have taken on the appearance
and warm patina of Alpine rock levigated by the monstrous
attrition of the glaciers. Where scistose rock was traversed by
a vein of quartz, which is much harder than its matrix, the
vein now protrudes, sometimes to an extent irritating to pedestrians with tender feet. Where, on the other hand, attrition
has been less or non-existent, one can distinguish the original
roughness of the stone and separate marks of the chisel can
still be seen: this is easily seen along the walls for about a
palm's breadth in length and especially well on the pavement
in front of Palazzo Carignano; the rectilinear stretch touching
the main entrance is eroded normally, whereas the recesses of
the baroque façade shelter rough slabs, because for more than
three centuries almost no one ever walked there.

Much more intense has been the wearing down of the
marble which is a less durable material: many thresholds of
old shops are made of marble and in the course of only a few
decades deep grooves have appeared in them. This erosion of
the thresholds is very noticeable in certain small mountain
churches or chapels, where for generations the faithful entered
wearing hob-nail boots. Often not only is the threshold worn

down but one also notices towards the interior a second hollowed out area at a distance of about fifty centimetres: it marks the almost obligatory point where the second footstep fell.

In front of many carriage gates one notices that the slab reveals a characteristic incision. From the two jambs extend two straight or curvilinear furrows diverging from each other; between them, parallel with the wall and about a dozen centimetres from each other, are traced more furrows along the entire length of the pavement. They were used to afford a grip for the iron shoes of the draft horses, those prehistoric animals: when the wagon ascended the connecting incline between the surface of the road and the pavement, the horses' hind legs were subjected to the greatest strain and would slip if the slab were smooth. The oldest among these incised slabs also showed the signs of wear caused by the iron rims and hoofs.

In various spots of the city the stone slabs preserve traces of the air raids during the Second World War. The slabs shattered by the exploding bombs have been replaced, but those which were pierced by incendiary bombs have been left in place. These devices were steel prisms which were dropped blindly by the aeroplanes and were so designed as to fall vertically, with so much impetus as to perforate roofs, attics, and ceilings; some of them falling on the pavements have neatly perforated the ten centimetre thick stone like a punch cutter. It is likely that anyone who would go to the trouble of lifting these perforated slabs would find the bomb's casing underneath; for example, two such perforations at a few metres' distance from each other can be found in front of No 9 bis on Corso Umberto. On seeing them one recalls the macabre rumours which circulated in wartime, about pedestrians who had not been quick enough to take shelter and had been pierced from head to foot.

Other signs are less sinister and more recent. Everywhere, but numerous in the more frequented sections, are certain round spots which can be seen on the slabs, spots having a diameter of a few centimetres, whiteish, grey or black. They are chewing gum, uncivilly spat on the ground and testify to the excellent mechanical properties of the material of which they are made: in fact if they are not removed (but removing them is not easy: it takes time and effort, not to mention the disgust, and the few store owners who go to the trouble of cleaning the pavement in front of their stores, know this all too well) they are practically indestructible. Their colour turns ever darker as their surface absorbs dust and grit, but they never disappear.

They constitute a good example of a phenomenon that one often encounters in technology: the effort made to establish the excellence of a particular material's resistance and solidity can often lead to serious difficulties when it comes to eliminating the material itself after it has fulfilled its functions; for example, it demanded an incredible effort to demolish the concrete fortifications of the Second World War; it is impossible to destroy glass and ceramic materials made to survive through the centuries; the ever longer lasting protective varnishes required by industry have led to the creation of a generation of solvents and varnish removers which are frighteningly aggressive. In the same way, the demand for a gum which resists, which changes form without being destroyed, and can undergo the torment of mastication, which consists in pressure, heat, humidity and enzymes, has resulted in a material which stands up only too well to trampling, rain, frost and the summer sun.

This gum, with its uselessly excellent performance, has found various secondary applications, all more or less noxious: and this too is a recurrent fact. It can be said that none of the tools for peace invented by man has escaped the fate of being used in the most harmful way, that is, as a weapon: scissors, hammers, scythes, pitchforks, mountain picks; even the short entrenching tools, as Remarque terrifyingly recounts in *All Quiet on the Western Front*. Chewing gum has not been used as a weapon but rather to sabotage the public transport ticket machines during the hottest months of juvenile confrontation.

As I said, chewed gum can be found everywhere, but a more attentive examination reveals that they reach maximum density in the vicinity of the most frequented bars and cafés: in fact the chewer who is headed there is forced to spit it out to free his mouth. As a result, an outsider, not familiar with the city, could find these places following the direction of the more thickly massed gum blobs, in the same way as sharks find their wounded prey by swimming in the direction of increasing concentrations of blood.

Alongside more obvious and trivial elements, these are the signs one sees on the pavement when the soul clings to it like chewing gum, because of sloth, laziness or fatigue.

# Against Pain

Many adolescents, perhaps all of them, are suddenly struck by an anguished doubt: 'All I know about the world has come to me through the senses: but what if the senses were deceiving me, as happens in dreams? If the stars, the sky, the past which I reconstruct through signs and the accounts of witnesses, the present of which I am aware, the persons I love and those I hate, the pain I feel, everything were the fruit of an unintended invention of mine and only I existed? If I were the centre of an infinite nothing, uselessly inhabited by the phantasms I evoke. There, I close my eyelids and stop my ears, and the universe is wiped out.'

As is known, this hypothesis is impervious to the attack of logic. It is coherent with itself, does not lead to contradictions, has been asserted by philosophers (but whom did they try to convince, since each one of them assumed he was the solitary worm in an illimitable apple?) and it has even been given the illustrious name of solipsism. Its innumerable inventors sooner or later end up by abandoning it (or forgetting it) for practical reasons; in fact it would lead to a most damaging behaviour for the person involved and his neighbour, that is, to inertia, renouncing the effort to influence the reality in which we are immersed. Moreover, one soon realises that this hypothesis, even though it can be held, is extremely improbable: it is improbable, for instance, that it is only by chance that my body is constantly identical to that of the individuals who populate the 'dream' of my daily encounters. In the same way, the hypothesis that the Earth is the immobile centre of the cosmos is not contradictory but improbable.

These centripetal considerations have returned to my mind when reading an article in defence of animals by E. Chiavacci, the moral theologian. I am in enthusiastic agreement with his conclusions, but some of his arguments leave me perplexed. A certain measure of suffering inflicted on animals is supposedly acceptable only because 'every animal is at the service of man': in fact, the creation is 'God's gift to man'. Also the Pleiades? Also Orion's nebula? A gift made to man fifteen billion years before he was born, and destined to survive at least as long again and after even the memory of our species will be extinguished?

Animals must be respected because 'God considers all creatures good', 'gives them food and protects them': how can one ignore the patient and cruel ambushes of spiders, the refined surgery with which (vivisection can't even compete!) certain wasps paralyse caterpillars, deposit a single egg inside them and go elsewhere to die, leaving the larva to slowly devour its still living host? Can one maintain that even here God 'prepares [for animals] a place of rest'? What shall we say about felines, those splendid killing machines? and about the perfidious cunning of the cuckoo bird, that murderer of his half-brothers as soon as he has left the egg? Certainly these creatures are not 'evil': but it seems necessary to admit that moral categories, good and evil, do not fit sub-humans. The gigantic sanguinary competition which was born with the first cell and which still unfolds around us stands outside or below our standards of behaviour.

Animals must indeed be respected, but for different reasons. Not because they are 'good' or useful to us (not all of them are), but because a rule written in us and recognised by all religions and all legislations commands us not to create pain, neither in ourselves nor in any creature capable of perceiving it. 'Everything is arcane but our pain.' The certitudes of the layman are few, but the first is this: suffering (and inflicting suffering) is acceptable only if rewarded by the avoidance of greater suffering to oneself or others.

It is a simple rule, but its consequences are complex, and everyone knows that. How to measure another's sufferings against one's own? But solipsism is a puerile fantasy: the 'others' do exist and among them are also the animals, our travelling companions. I do not believe that the life of a raven or a grasshopper is worth the same as a human life; it is doubtful whether an insect perceives pain as we do, but birds probably perceive it and certainly mammals. It is the difficult task of every man to diminish as much as he can the tremendous bulk of this substance which contaminates every life – pain in all its forms; it is strange but beautiful that this imperative is reached even when starting from radically different presuppositions.

# Thirty Hours on
## *Castoro Sei*

The thirty hours on *Castoro Sei* (*Beaver Six*) in April 1980 were a rare gift to a landlubber like myself, a man for whom the sea is the sea of vacations in Liguria and the transfigured sea which emerges from the pages of Coleridge, Conrad, Verne, and Melville. And it was especially to these last two that my memory continually returned during that all too brief sojourn of mine: more precisely to *Twenty Thousand Leagues Under the Sea*, and in particular to the guided tour that Captain Nemo offers Monsieur Aronnax through the mechanical bowels of the *Nautilus*, and to a sentence (which has stuck in my mind for over thirty years) of Cesare Pavese, the translator in his preface to *Moby Dick*: '. . . Melville . . . knows much more about life than the Vatican [libraries] and the pavement bookstalls, and he knows that the best poems are told by illiterate sailors in the forecastle.'

These two references, or should I say these two literary pretexts, are worth what all such references are worth. The sailors of the *Castoro* are anything but illiterate: on the contrary they are sailor-engineers, a human species which in Melville's time did not exist but which Verne, however, had foreseen and anticipated with that mysterious intuition of a technological seer that allowed him to foresee fifty or one hundred years ahead of time the use in warfare of helicopters, television, a missile with its human crew flung at the moon (precisely from Cape Canaveral!) and the after all quite plausible submarine.

Captain Pietro Costanzo will forgive me if I have here

compared him to Captain Nemo, misanthropic, vindictive, and
devilish, nor in any case is the *Castoro* a submarine: but, like
the *Nautilus*, its belly is packed with wonders. Like the submar-
ines (and, besides, technically it is precisely defined as a 'semi-
submersible') and like the whaling ships of olden times and
today, it is a non-ship, a ship for which navigating is an
implicit and lateral activity but which in substance is meant
for other, more definite uses. The devices it contains arouse
wonder exactly because of the extreme refinement with which
they serve a precise and unusual aim: to deposit on the bottom
of the sea from Tunisia to Sicily at depths never until then
reached a rigid steel pipe covered with cement, manipulating it
as if it were light and flexible as a rubber tube.

The history of technology demonstrates that, when it is
faced by new problems, scientific education and precision are
necessary but insufficient. Two other virtues are needed, and
they are experience and inventive imagination, but in the trade
of the exploitation of natural gases, which is very recent,
experience does not extend through centuries or millennia: it is
compressed within decades, or even briefer periods. It is much
shorter than a human life, and fathers have nothing they can
teach their sons; it cannot count on that slow, almost Dar-
winian evolution which has moulded firearms over the course
of five centuries, and the automobile in the course of one.
Experience needs trials and errors, but here there is no time to
make mistakes and correct them, and imagination must prevail,
which works by leaps, at a fast clip, through radical and rapid
mutations. But nothing of valid experiences is lost, even the
most remote; just as our body has inherited the genetic mechanism and proteic architecture of monocellular organisms, and
just as the automobile incorporates the design of the horse-
drawn wagon, so in *Castoro Sei* we recognise interesting and
illustrious innovative ideas which go back to the dawn of our
civilisation: the house on stilts, the double hull of the catamaran.
This, too, is worth meditating on, like philosophy's great
ideas and great problems (whether matter is infinitely divisible;

whether the universe is finite or infinite, eternal or transient; whether our will is free or determined), so also great technical inventions are transformed but do not die. The lever, the wheel, the roof survive the millennia; no metal has fallen into disuse and on the contrary innumerable new uses have been found for the most ancient metals; it would be difficult to mention an obsolete plastic material, while the oldest among them, phenolic resins and polystyrene, have lost none of their importance.

The same argument can be made regarding the men on board the *Castoro*. Just as the vessel is singular and unique in the world, so is the make-up of its crew; or rather its crews, because there are three sections of one hundred and fifty men each, which follow each other in rotation, two on board (for twenty-eight days, Sundays and holidays included, with twelve working hours a day and twelve of rest) and one crew on land and on vacation for fourteen days. It is a composite crew; it includes welders, mechanics, electricians, electronic specialists, crane operators, engineers, finishers, mechanists, labourers, not to mention the men in charge of services and navigation. Nevertheless, the separation (the 'inter-face') between sailors and workers and at a higher level between officers and engineers is not clearcut because the navigation of the *Castoro* is a strange type of navigation.

What is normally called a ship is expected to navigate quickly in a longitudinal direction, and only exceptionally in reverse. The *Castoro* however, sails forward only when it is moving from place to place; but in truth to speak of backward or forward, in the *Castoro* case, does not make much sense: she does not have a true and proper prow, the extremity from which the pipe descends into the water, which therefore moves backwards during the pipe-laying operation, is by convention called the prow. She can move in all directions because she has four movable propellers fixed at the four corners of the hull's underside. As a rule she does not exceed the speed of six or seven knots; for this ship, which is in fact a most sophisticated floating workshop, stability and positioning are much more important than speed. In other words, she must be able to remain in one place in respect to the marine bottom – that is, the pipe – within a margin of a few feet. It must not oscillate with the motion of the waves, must not respond to wind and currents, and when she moves to lay the pipe she must do so at an exactly regulated speed. For this to take place with the due reliability a refined system of automation has been resorted to which, at each 'launching' of the pipe, dictates to the twelve winches of the twelve anchors (formidable anchors that weigh from twenty to twenty-five tons each), and to the four engine groups, the movements necessary for the pipe to descend into the water without being subjected to stresses exceeding those permitted by the resistance and specifications of the materials involved. The moment of 'launching', that is, the advancing of the pipe, which is repeated (if everything proceeds according to plan) approximately every ten minutes, is an unforgettable spectacle: at the command of the electronic brain which directs the operation, the colossal winches start up simultaneously, those at the poop pulling in the cable, those at the prow releasing it, and the forty thousand tons of the *Castoro Sei* ponderously moves towards the Sicilian coast for exactly twelve metres, that is, the length of one section of pipe: but the movement is so smooth and without sudden jerks that those on board do not perceive it. One sees only the tube gliding forward and has the impression that it is the tube that moves and the ship that stands still. This is a concrete illustration of Galilean relativity, and Dante's Garisenda also comes to mind, which seems to bend towards the earth when the clouds driven by the wind move against its background.

Automation is a young art, and it is natural that young men are in charge of it; but also those who are older have often proved to be valuable: their experience accumulated over the course of the years even in much different kinds of work has proven of great value in handling the unexpected; in fact, it would be naïve to think that in so complex a system, destined

to operate under such unusual conditions, it is possible to
foresee everything and accidents never occur. I was told of two
episodes, indeed two unexpected events, which prove how
much previous experience and inventive imagination still are
valuable when it is a matter of solving a new problem quickly
and 'with the means on board'.

The basis of the *Castoro*'s work is welding. She is in
substance a welding workshop almost one hundred and fifty
metres long; along the pipe which gradually advances by
degrees there are posted eight successive welding stations, and
the joining of the pipe sections is performed, in part automatically and in part manually, and in accordance with highly
sophisticated welding techniques. Before the launch, and at the
end of the welding operation, a control by X-ray must be
performed; if the weld is perfect the pipe continues to advance;
if it reveals flaws, these are rapidly eliminated. The X-ray
generator is contained in a trolley mounted on wheels which
runs inside the pipe, or, more properly, is in a fixed position in
respect to the ship, while the enveloping pipe moves past it;
this apparatus is fastened to a cable and because of its elongated shape it was called the 'piglet'. In the course of the
work, for some reason which has remained mysterious, the
'piglet' suddenly disappeared: the cable had snapped, the trolley
had gone down the pipe's incline, and the very costly apparatus
had descended for a length of three hundred metres. The
damage was serious: apart from the forced interruption of the
launching operation (I have been told that *one minute* of
*Castoro Sei*'s work costs two hundred and eighty thousand
lire!) the 'piglet' almost completely obstructed the pipe and
had at all costs to be quickly removed.

A summit meeting of technicians was called and various
proposals were made, among which the most picturesque was
the following: make a phone call to Tunisia, have a ball made
of rubber or some other elastic material put into the pipe, and
pump behind it compressed air as is done with pneumatic tube
mail. The ball would reach the 'piglet' at the bottom of the

Mediterranean and shoot it out. The discussion was still going on when a member of the crew came forward; he was an ex-fisherman, and to him it seemed obvious that the 'piglet' must be fished out. His proposal did not seem that easy to put into effect, but it was simple, quick, and cost only a few thousand lire; the man was taken to the workshop where he had a large hook made and attached a weight to it. He introduced hook and weight into the mouth of the pipe and after a few minutes of patient attempts snagged the 'piglet' and pulled it out.

The second episode is on a Cyclopean scale. As mentioned, the positioning and progress of the *Castoro* rest on a complex anchoring system. The twelve gigantic anchors are set in a circle around the ship, and as a rule the ship 'walks' on its twelve anchors; when as she moves, pulled by the cables, she comes too close to the anchors on the Sicilian side, these are lifted and dropped again further on, and those on the Tunisian side are brought closer to the ship. The times, angles, and distances of the anchors' repositioning are dictated by the computer on board, and the operation is performed by tugs which follow and surround the *Castoro* like solicitous attendants. The mooring hawsers (of steel, three inches in diameter) are two thousand, seven hundred metres long: when all is said and done, the *Castoro*, its anchors, each marked by its buoy, the tugs, and the supply boats which shuttle back and forth to land and supply the *Castoro* with pipes, fuel, etc. occupy several square kilometres of sea.

During a night of fierce tempest one of the just mentioned buoys disappeared; it was impossible to locate with precision the anchor it had marked and so move it when its turn came. Apparently the buoy had somehow been damaged: it was the unsinkable type, but its floating power had been reduced and the weight of the cable that tied it to the anchor held it under water in an unspecified spot both as to its location and depth from the surface. This too was a fishing problem, but fishing blindly; and the anchor resting on the bottom weighed twenty-five tons plus at least another ten for the chain. And it was solved, indeed, as a blind man would have solved it, that is, by groping. From one of the tugs a large hook was slipped under the cable, visible for a few metres, which went from the *Castoro* to the anchor; then the tug began to move, through a frightful sea, letting the hook run along the cable but always keeping the rope taut to which the hook was fastened. The hook was let down on a slant, following links of the cable for a depth of almost two kilometres down to the enormous links of the chain that connects the cable to the anchor; the first link was caught, and the tug's powerful winch lifted the anchor and chain high enough for the damaged buoy to rise to the surface again.

So here are the 'poems' to which Pavese alluded when speaking of Melville. They were not told to me in the forecastle (which I do not think exists on the *Castoro*), but at the mess table in front of a glass of good wine; and not by illiterate soldiers, but rather by Captain Costanzo and the other men of the crew, young and not so young, cybernetic engineers at their first encounter with the working world, machinists, proud of every single bolt of their machines, sailor-workers who in this unusual and colossal undertaking have again discovered the ancient virtues of competence put to the test and of work well done. I hope that they will not be surprised nor shocked if their accounts seemed poetic to me. In fact, in their controlled, educated, precise and unrhetorical words I have recognised the echo of the voice of another navigator and storyteller whose remote adventures are today eternal poetry: the navigator who journeyed for ten years across strange seas and whose prime virtues, much more than courage, which he had in abundance, were patience and multifarious ingenuity.

# The Hidden Player

I did not want any games: I can produce trustworthy witnesses. I have owned a word processor for a whole year now; it has almost become part of my body, as happens with shoes, glasses, or dentures; I absolutely need it to write and file; but I did not want it to take me over, and so I did not want to let frivolous programmes into the house. The computer was supposed to be used for work, and that's all. Instead the unforeseeable (or foreseeable) took place, I have received the gift of a programme for chess playing and have yielded to the seduction.

Let's be clear, playing chess is not a frivolous undertaking for chess players, or generally for those who devote themselves to this game with seriousness and passion; but for me it is. I play rather badly: I lack the fundamental qualities, the ability to concentrate, the logical power, the specific memory and culture, and the tenacity. But I play anyway, precisely in a frivolous and reckless manner, at long and irregular intervals, without bothering to learn the classic openings and closings. I play when the right kind of adversary comes within reach (it happens ever more infrequently), an adversary who plays more or less like me, with the same dreamy and festive spirit, and at a level not too different from mine: otherwise if he's too good, he squashes me like an ant, and if he's too weak my victory is insipid and similar to taking sweets from a baby. This is the only game which I have accepted and to which I have remained faithful: all others bore me, I am upset when I lose, but do not feel any joy when I win. I have accepted it for remote dynastic reasons: in an obscure way, the old household chess board contains our Lares; it is perhaps the only object that was materially transmitted from father to son. For I don't know how many generations every ancestor of mine has taught his son the rules, and has defeated him for a few years, then has tacitly admitted his son's superiority. I do not mean to say that the level is improving from generation to generation: it is the talent for chess which reaches its apex around the age of twenty and then as one grows older decreases – a sad but natural fact.

Now the electronic player has burst on to this traditional scene. Having rendered due homage to the confraternity of excellent brains that have programmed it, the comparison is obligatory: which is the more desirable opponent? Man or machine? The answer cannot help but be vague, indeed evanescent: a comparison should be made between comparable terms, and these two are not. But let's try anyhow.

The machine is always there, at any moment of day or night, one does not have to invite it over or go to his house, it is always at your disposal, it doesn't get tired, it doesn't get nervous, it doesn't try to get you nervous (as human chess players, especially extremely good ones are notoriously known to do). You can assign it various levels: choose, that is, an opponent of a ranking equal to yours. There is a certain price to pay for this, however, at least with my programme: the more skilful your antagonist is, the longer he makes you wait for his move. Now, a five-minute wait in front of a human opponent is tolerable: you look him in the face while his eyes are fixed on the board, try to read in it his intentions or at least his state of mind. The machine instead is hermetic: it too 'thinks' for all the time you've given it, but of its very rapid review of the possible decisions there appears on the screen alongside the chess board nothing more than an illegible swarming of figures, a sequence of hypotheses following one another, too swift (five or ten a second) for the eye to be able to follow. Its five minutes are very long.

As I said, you can choose a counterpart who plays well, not so well, or badly: in each case it plays with a style that is not human. Man has flashes of illumination (not only at the chess board!) in which he surpasses himself and which can be translated into inspired moves, those which in customary notation are accompanied by one or even two exclamation marks; but he also has moments of distraction (these on the contrary carry a question mark), whose frequency increases towards the end of the game and a chess player's career. The machine is flat: it does not make exclamatory moves, but it is never distracted, and never grows old.

This does not mean that it does not make mistakes; it does, and it always makes the same mistakes: I have noticed for instance, that it is precipitously avid, if there is one of your pieces to be taken it swoops down to grab it, even if on the other half of the board its ruination is being prepared. These evidently are gaps in the programme: once you identify them and learn to exploit them, you win the game, but also the pleasure of playing has vanished.

You're offered an exciting menu of services, which are, so to speak, accessory. The match can be recorded: if it is very good, you can play it over again and relive all its emotions. You can interrupt it at any moment and go back to it when you wish. If you are in doubt about what to do, you can ask the machine for advice and it will answer you in the most loyal and chivalrous manner. If, like me, your openings are weak (chess players worthy of the name know them by heart), you can ask the machine to cancel them from its assortment to balance your handicap. At each move a score appears on the screen, which expresses the situation on the basis of complicated parameters. If it is positive, it indicates that things are not going well for you, if it goes over five hundred you would do well to withdraw; if it goes over one thousand, catastrophe is near at hand.

A negative score symmetrically indicates that you are the winner by a material advantage or position. Of course, if this mute commentator embarrasses you, you can get rid of it. You can even ask the machine to play against itself: and the spectacle has something hallucinatory about it, because the match that unfolds in silence before your eyes is never the same. The whimsical talents who created the programme have introduced a margin of indetermination, a bit of 'free will', so that in an identical situation the machine does not always act in an identical fashion.

The hidden mechanical player (whose almost human intelligence is contained in a small disk which weighs only a few grams) is therefore a great seducer, he is there waiting for you, always ready and always new, polite and ruthless. He beckons, calls you, distracts you from work and also from reading, but he is not human. You can admire his expertise, as one admires the dancing Lippizaner horses, or the seals in the circus; you can even, illicitly, feel a curious kind of compassion for him – for at bottom he is only a little disk – when you see him faced by an intricate situation; but a flesh and blood opponent is qualitatively different.

He is your blood brother, even if you met him only a few hours ago. You see his face, you measure yourself against him, you know him to be as capable as you are of happy inventions and off-the-wall mistakes. At the end of the match, as if at the end of a life, you can talk to him with the familiarity that is born from a contest, comment on his mistakes and yours, judge him and feel judged by him. He learns ('sadly learns') from you and you from him, whereas the machine already knows everything and learns nothing. Nevertheless, you can still learn something from it: even if only patience and attention, and (why not?) the theory of game endings.

# Ritual and Laughter

There are those who write to astonish, indeed, there have been periods when evoking wonder in the reader was considered the prime aim of the writing trade; but the book that amazed me most and which I came across by chance certainly had not been written for this purpose. It is a book on the subject of religion, or, more precisely, ritual, and I am not religious; but I will not comment on it with a critical intention, because I respect the believer and sometimes envy him. Its bizarre aspects have led me to think: they have taken me back to a way of conceiving life and the world which is far from ours, but must be understood if we want to understand ourselves, and which it would be foolish to liquidate with mockery.

The book is called *Shulkhan Arukh* (*The Set Table*); it was written in Hebrew (but I read it in translation) in the sixteenth century by a Spanish rabbi; although it has considerable bulk, it is the compendium of many preceding works and in substance contains the rules, customs and beliefs of the Judaism of his time. It is divided into four parts which respectively deal with: the daily precepts, the Sabbath, and holidays; food, money, purity and mourning; marriage; rabbinical, civil and penal legislation. The author, Joseph Caro, was Sephardic and did not know the rules and customs of Eastern Jews; therefore the text was subsequently revised by the famous Rabbi Moses Isserles of Cracow, who wrote a commentary on it amusingly entitled *The Tablecloth*, with which he proposed to fill the gaps and make it suitable for the Askenazi reader.

As we know, Jews are forbidden to pronounce the 'true' name of God: actually it is printed in books, but when reading it must be replaced by synonyms. As a rule it is permissible to pronounce the word 'God' in languages other than Hebrew (but I have known a German Jew who, out of extreme reverence and for fear of sinning, in his letters wrote *Gtt* instead of *Gott*: the same is done by the few Italian followers of the Rabbi Lubavich who write *D-o* instead of *Dio*), and at any rate the authors of *The Set Table* and *The Tablecloth* are concerned about what can take place at the public bath where the presence of human bodies makes the environment intensely profane; therefore at the bath it is preferable not to pronounce the name of God, 'not even in German or Polish'. As we see, this is certainly a gloss by Isserles: and in any case it does not appear that in 1500 in Spain public baths were widespread. For similar reasons, in closing a letter one must not write 'adiós', 'adio', 'adieu': the letter might get smudged or wind up in the rubbish-bin.

The concept of nudity is vast, chiefly as regards women: any portion of the body that is usually covered is nudity, and so is the hair. In short, nudity is everything that might attract the attention of men, distracting him from the thought of God: so 'the voice of a singing woman' is also considered the same as nudity.

We also notice the same extremist tendency 'to erect a hedge' about the law at all costs with regard to the prohibition against working on the Sabbath. The fundamental tasks of rural and artisan life of the time are amplified with untrammelled imagination. The pressing of grapes is forbidden: hence also any kind of 'squeezing', for example, one is not allowed to squeeze fruit; but if the liquid obtained is to be thrown away, then squeezing is permitted, and one may squeeze and drain salad. It is forbidden to hunt: what to do about a flea? One can catch it and fling it far away, but one mustn't kill it. Hunting is also catching, trapping: so before closing a case or trunk you must make sure that it does not contain flies or moths; if you were to shut them in there, you would be hunting, without having either the will or consciousness, and you would have broken the Sabbath.

How will you conduct yourself if on the Sabbath you should realise that your tub is leaking? You cannot plug the hole because that would be servile work, nor can you explicitly ask a servant or a Christian friend to see to it, because making others work is also forbidden. Even less can you offer to recompense someone on the morrow because this would be a contract, and contracts are also forbidden on the Sabbath.

This is the suggested solution: if the damage threatens to be serious, you may say impersonally: 'If someone were to repair this, he would not be sorry.'

On the day of rest and merriment it is also forbidden to write and cancel, perhaps in memory of the time when writing was done by carving stone. This prohibition is the source of a fantastically ramified casuistry. One cannot trace letters or doodle on a misted-over pane of glass; in handling a book one must be careful not to mark its cover with one's nails; on the other hand, it is permissible to eat a cake that bears writing or decorations. To sweep is abrading, and therefore by a bold expansion of the concept it comes under the heading of forbidden work because it involves cancelling: but it is permissible to do it 'in a non-habitual fashion', for example, using goose feathers instead of a broom. It is forbidden to light a fire and also to extinguish it. Naturally it is permitted, indeed obligatory, to extinguish a fire on the Sabbath if human lives are in danger; but 'if clothes catch fire one can pour water on the part which is not burning, yet not directly on the fire'.

Idolatry must be held in abomination. One must not even look at idols, nor may one get closer to them and must stay at a distance from them of at least four cubits. If, in passing close to an idol you step on a thorn, you must not bend over to remove it because to some this might look like a gesture of homage: but you mustn't bend even if nobody's there because the act might seem such to yourself later on, in memory. You must move away, or sit down, or at least turn your back to the idol.

As regards the prohibition against eating meat and milk together, hypotheses and solutions are formulated that remind one of the studies and problems of chess players: that is, elegantly improbable situations are imagined, abstract but useful for subtle reasoning. If two pious Jews eat at the same table, and one eats meat and the other dairy products they must draw a line on the tablecloth to divide the two areas, or at any rate make a border. They must not drink from the same glass because bits of food could cling to it. If together with the meat one prepares a dish with almond 'milk', some whole almonds must be left in it, so that it is clear that it is not real milk.

What should we say about this labyrinth? The product of other times? Wasted time and ingenuity? Degradation of religious feeling to massive regulation? Is this *Set Table* to be thrown away, forgotten, or defended? And if it is to be defended, how should it be? I do not believe that one can dismiss this book and in general the ritual with a shrug of one's shoulders, as we do with many things that do not concern us. The ritual, every ritual, is condensed history and pre-history: it is a core with a fine and complex structure, it is an enigma to be solved; if solved, it will help us to solve other enigmas which touch us more closely. And after all, the names are also something.

But besides all this, I feel in this *Table* a fascination which is for all time, the fascination of *subtilitas*, the disinterested game of the intellect: to split hairs in four is not the trade of an idler but rather mental training. Behind these curious pages I perceive an ancient taste for bold discussion, an intellectual flexibility that does not fear contradictions, indeed welcomes them as an inevitable ingredient of life; and life is rule, it is order prevailing over Chaos, but the rule has crevices, unexplored pockets of exception, license, indulgence and disorder. Trouble is in store for anyone who cancels them, perhaps they contain the germ of all our tomorrows, because the machine of the universe is subtle, subtle are the laws which rule it, and every year the rules obeyed by sub-atomic particles reveal themselves to be more and more subtle. Einstein's words have often been quoted: 'The Lord is subtle, but he is not wicked'; hence subtle must be, in His likeness, those who follow Him. One notes that among physicists and cyberneticists there are many Jews from Eastern Europe: could their *esprit de finesse* be a Talmudic inheritance?

But above all, under its stern crust I hear in this *Table* a laughter I like: it is the same laughter in Jewish jokes where the rules are boldly turned upside down, and it is the laughter of us 'modern' readers. Whoever wrote that pinching a flea is hunting, or opening on the Sabbath a book that has something written on its spine is *probably* not permissible must have laughed as he wrote just as we laugh as we read: he was not different from us even if he was concerned with distinguishing between permissible and impermissible work and we concern ourselves with financial statements, mixed concrete, or alphanumeric codes.

# The Need for Fear

Almost all of us are afraid of earwigs: I mean those brown insects with a flattened and elongated body whose abdomen ends in a pincer that looks menacing. They hide beneath the bark of trees, or sometimes nest in clothes warmed by the sun, and in the folds of umbrellas or deck chairs. They do not harm anyone: the pincer is not poisonous, and in fact does not pince at all (it is an organ that facilitates mating); and it is not true, yet is tenaciously taught from generation to generation, that 'if you aren't careful they slip into your ears'. This notion is so rooted in our collective memory that it has been received in the binary denomination of the little animal, which in fact is officially called 'Forficula auriculara'; but the English and Germans did not wait for the scientific baptism and have for centuries called it, respectively, 'earwig' and 'Ohrwurm', the insect or worm of the ear. Besides the pincer, the earwig has another property that inspires in us a strange fear: like all nocturnal animals, if it is exposed to light, it goes abruptly from immobility to flight, and its being startled is reflected in our being startled.

All women and men are afraid of bats. This too is a localised and falsely motivated fear: 'They plunge into your hair, and since they have hook-shaped claws, you cannot shake them loose'; not by chance also bats are nocturnal animals and have an irregular flight based on restless and sudden turns. Now, our native bats, unarmed and harmless, are afraid of man, never go near him nor let him come near them; but our racist aversion to 'bad people, people who roam about at night' (thus Don Abbondio) does not retreat when faced by a complete absence of experimental confirmation. Anyone who is abroad at night is bad by definition, and in his most popular image the Devil, when he has wings, has the wings of a bat, whereas fairies have butterfly wings and angels the wings of a swan. Perhaps our enmity for the bat is reinforced by his distant relationship with the infamous vampires: but vampires, real vampires, not those of the black legends of the Carpathians, are in turn almost harmless; the amount of blood that they extract in one session (rarely at the expense of man) is not a twentieth part of what we donate to the volunteer blood donors' association gladly and without any harm to us, without indeed even noticing its loss.

All women and many men are horrified by mice and rats, which are also nocturnal and furtive. Do you remember Winston, the main character of Orwell's terrifying *1984*? He endures ferocious tortures with dignity, but surrenders and betrays his woman ('Do it to Julia! Not me! . . . Strip her to the bones'), when his torturer threatens to bring a rat close to his face. No one who rereads that page can have any doubts: the obsessive fear that Orwell attributes to his character is *his* fear, a phobia, perfectly compatible with the admirable courage the writer has shown throughout his life in peace and war. For Winston, and for Orwell, 'the worst thing in the world happens to be rats'. The absurd and picturesque justification (anatomical like the two preceding ones) which popular mythology offers for this phobia is well known: rats love holes, and if they can they slip into the intestines or up the female genitals.

I do not believe that in order to interpret these and other atavistic fears we must turn to psychoanalysis, which in the hands of dilettantes lends itself so well to explaining all mental phenomena and their opposites after the fact, and is so ill suited to seeing them ahead of time. There is nothing archetypal or congenital here, and it seems to me that we can be satisfied with a simpler key: in all cultures there are dangers, true, presumed, or exaggerated which are transmitted by the fathers (or, more often, by the mothers) to the children, along chains of innumerable generations, and which create as many fears. The fact that some people are immune to this proves nothing: every individual has predispositions or defences. At any rate, the same transmission of fear takes place among cattle: the mother cows when they see their offspring approach poisonous hellebores to eat them, push them away with a toss of their horns; but precisely because there does not exist a bovine 'culture', only the prohibitions and rules dictated by experience are handed down and not those which spring from intellectual construction.

Bordering this vast region of traditional fears (not only of animals: when I was a child I was forbidden by some forgotten governess to touch ranunculi 'because they make your finger-nails fall out') is the fear of snakes; perhaps beyond the border, since in fact there are also in Italy snakes with a fatal bite. They are only three or four species of vipers, but it seems that their population is increasing because of the abandonment of farming in the mountains, and because of the foolish extermination of the predatory birds which are their natural antagonists. There are indeed such poisonous snakes, no matter what extremist ecologists may say, who at all costs postulate a friendly and mild nature, and they are not a negligible danger, especially for children; but around the nucleus of the silent and deadly beast which slithers on its belly an intense emotional aura and a swarm of legends has formed over the millennia.

The snake in the flesh, like all other animals, is not a subject for morality: it is neither good nor bad, it devours and is devoured. It occupies various ecological niches, and its structure, so (apparently) simple and so unusual, is the outcome of a very long and not linear evolutionary history: in fact, like the cetaceans it had four limbs which it 'realised' it could do without and of which it sometimes preserves the rudiments in its skeleton. It has patented several ingenious and specific devices: a 'thermic eye' sensitive to infra-red rays, that is, to the heat emitted by birds and mammals which only recently (and for the same purpose: to locate a victim at night) man has managed to imitate; a mandible that it can disarticulate at will, so as to permit the introduction of voluminous prey in its stomach: and in the poisonous species, a double syringe with lightning-like effects.

The literary serpent is on the contrary morally singled out: right from the first pages of *Genesis* where it appears as the most cunning of animals and the inciter to the original sin. It is evil and accursed and its slithering is at once punishment and symbol. For the ancients, man's verticality was the sign of his almost divine nature: he reaches towards the sky, he is the hyphen between the earth and the stars. Quadrupeds are something intermediary, they are prone, their gaze is directed at the ground, but they are separated from the ground: they run, jump. The snake adheres to the earth, is earth, eats earth (*Genesis*, 4.14), like the worm of which he is an enlarged version, and the worm is the child of putrescence.

The snake is the beast *par excellence*, the one that does not harbour anything human in itself: significantly, the Italian word 'biscia' (grass snake) is nothing but a variant of the Latin and Italian 'bestia' (beast), and the no-legged is felt to be more distant from us than ants, crickets, or spiders, who do have legs (too many perhaps, and with too many knees). Punctually, Dante identifies the snake with the thief who, like it, glides soundlessly, and at night insinuates itself into man's houses; and in the seventh circle thieves and snakes are endlessly transformed into each other. In La Fontaine's two hundred and thirty-seven fables the wolf appears fifteen times, the lion seventeen, and the fox nineteen, and they are intensely humanised in their vices and virtues; the snake appears only three times and in marginal and vaguely allusive roles.

As far as I remember, literature's only 'positive' snake is Kipling's python Kaa. Kaa, Flathead, is wise, prudent, vain, and as old as the jungle, but he finds a new youth every time he changes his very beautiful skin. He is Mowgli's friend, but at a distance: a cold-blooded friend, clever and incomprehensible, from whom Frog the man-cub can learn much but of whom he must always beware.

There are not many snakes in my personal history. I once was standing on the small piazza of a village. I was holding my young son in my arms, and in front of me some chickens were scrabbling; from the beak of one of them hung a shoestring. Every now and then she would lay it down on the ground, then she picked it up again jealously if she saw one of the flock approach to take it away from her. Suddenly I noticed that the shoelace was moving: it was a small snake, by now in a pretty bad state because of all the pecking. I felt the Biblical hatred reawaken in me: it was a serpent, therefore a viper, therefore it had to be killed. I flung the child into the arms of the first passerby, and amid the astonishment of those present, ran after the chicken, she, too, amazed and rightly indignant. After a brief joust, I managed to seize the already condemned victim, and I trampled on it with the pure conscience of one who knows that he is fulfilling his duty as a father and as a citizen. Today I would no longer do this, or at least I would give it a moment's thought: vipers, even if in good health, are much less swift than popular zoology claims and therefore less dangerous.

Perhaps we have a deep need for these false fears, half-way between reality and play-acting and games, the fear of mice, ranunculi, and spiders. They are our way of falling in line with tradition, proving ourselves to be the children of the culture in which we have grown up; or perhaps they help us relegate to the shadows other closer and vaster fears.

# To a Young Reader

Dear Sir,

I hope you will forgive me if I answer your letter of ...
publicly, omitting of course your name and whatever else
could reveal your identity. However, for the benefit of all
those who are in your situation, or in a similar situation, and
who like you have written to me, I am forced to reveal at least
this: that you are twenty-seven years old, live in a small town,
have finished classical *liceo* without excessive efforts, and have
now with great difficulty found a modest job which gives you
a little money, a certain security and scant gratification.

You want to write, and more precisely to tell stories; and in
fact you do write but want advice and orientation from me:
how to write. You do not pose for me, and do not pose for
yourself the fundamental dilemma, that is, whether to write or
not, and in so doing put me in an awkward position from the start.
In fact, from what you tell me one must assume that you think of
storytelling as a trade, whereas in my opinion it is not.

In Italy, today, every trade coincides with a guarantee: he
who lives on writing has no guarantees. As a consequence, pure
storytellers, those who gain their living from their creativity
alone, are very few: they are not more than a couple of dozen.
The others write in their spare time, devoting the rest of their
time to publicity, journalism, publishing, the cinema, teaching,
or other activities that have nothing to do with writing. So in
the first place I suggest, indeed, I prescribe that you hold on to
your job.

If you truly have the blood of a writer, you will find the time for writing no matter what, it will grow around you: and, for all that, your daily work, boring though it may be, cannot help but supply you with precious raw materials for your evening or Sunday writing, beginning with human contacts, beginning with boredom itself. Boredom is boring by definition, but a discourse on boredom can be a vital and exciting exercise for the reader: you who have studied the classics in school certainly already know this.

But you skip this fork in the road and yet expect from me practical and specific advice: the secrets of the trade, indeed, the non-trade. They exist, I cannot deny it, but luckily they have no general validity; I say 'luckily' because, if they did, all writers would write in the same way, thus generating such an enormous mass of boredom as to render vain any attempt to pass it off as Leopardian, and to trip the automatic switches of the most indulgent readers due to over-load. Therefore I will have to confine myself to telling you my personal secrets, at the risk of forming with my own hands the competitor who, despite my 'introduction', will chase me out of the market. The first secret is the rest period in the drawer, and I believe it has a general value. Between the first draft and the final one a few days must pass; for reasons which I do not know, for a certain period of time the eye of the writer is not very sensitive to the recent text. It is necessary, so to speak, for the ink to dry well; before that, the flaws elude you: repetitions, logical gaps, improprieties, grating, off-key notes.

An excellent surrogate for the rest period can be a guinea-pig reader endowed with common sense and good taste, not too indulgent: one's spouse, a friend. Not another writer: a writer is not a typical reader, he has preferences and peculiar fixations, faced by a beautiful text he is envious. I am contravening this rest period concept at this very moment, because as soon as I have written this letter I shall mail it; so you will be able to verify its validity.

After the ripening period, which assimilates a piece of

writing to wine, perfumes and medlars, there comes the time to decant, refine. One almost always realises that one has sinned by excess, that the text is redundant, repetitive, prolix: or at least, I repeat, that's what happens to me. Incorrigibly, in the first draft I address myself to an obtuse reader, who has to have the concepts hammered into his head. After the thinning down, the writing is more agile: it approaches what, more or less consciously, is my goal, that of maximum information with minimum clutter.

Take note that one can attain the maximum of information by various paths, some quite subtle; one, fundamental, is the choice of synonyms which are almost never equivalent to each other. There is always one which is 'more right' than the others: but often it is necessary to look for it, depending on the context, in the old Tommaseo, or among the neologisms of the new Zingarelli, or among the barbarisms stupidly prohibited by the traditionalists, even among the terms of other languages; if there is no Italian term, why go in for contortions?

In this research, it seems to me important to keep alive the awareness of the original meaning of each word; if, for example, you remember that 'to unleash' meant to free from leashes (bonds), you will be able to use the term in a more appropriate manner and in less threadbare senses. Not all readers will notice the artifice, but they will at least perceive that the choice wasn't obvious, that you have worked for them, that you have not followed the line of least resistance.

After ninety years of psychoanalysis, and successful or failed attempts to pour the unconscious directly on to the page, I have an acute need for clarity and rationality, and I think that the majority of readers feel the same way. A clear text is not *per force* elementary; it can be read at several levels, but the lowest level, in my opinion, should be accessible to a broad public. Do not be afraid of doing an injustice to your id by gagging it, there is no danger, 'the tenant on the floor below' will find a way to show up in any case, because writing means laying oneself bare: even the cleanest writer bares himself. If you do not like to bare yourself, be satisfied with your present job. Oh, I forgot to tell you that, in order to write, one must have something to write.

With best regards, your

Primo Levi

# IF NOT NOW, WHEN?

*Primo Levi*

*'If I'm not for myself, who will be for me?*
*If not this way, how? If not now, when?'*

So runs the *Song of the Partisan*. This enthralling novel
pays tribute to the Jews who fought back during the
holocaust. Based on a true story, it chronicles the
adventures, crises and moral struggles of a group of
Russian and Polish refugees as, stranded in occupied
territory, they offer what resistance they can to the
German army.

'This book achieves many things – too many, really, to
itemise . . . yet one is left with an enormous sense of
optimism and gratitude to the author' *The Listener*

'Levi writes of unimaginable hardships: cold above all,
pain, terror, hunger and weariness, exclusion from
humanity, an almost wolfish sense of exile in marshes and
forests, sewers, caves, collapsed buildings. And of
exhilaration, commitment, hope, the longing for a home'
*Financial Times*

'Levi is a master whose hand never slips . . . I was
convinced by every detail, and absurdly shaken to realise
at the end that it was indeed fiction, however well
grounded in fact. I knew these people, and I wanted to
know more' *The Times*

0 349 12199 0
FICTION

# THE WRENCH
## *Primo Levi*

'This is not a book for journalists. Civil servants, too, will feel uneasy while reading it, and as for lawyers, they will never sleep again. For it is about a man in his capacity as homo faber, a maker of things with his hands, and what has any of us ever made but words. I say it is "about" the man who makes; truly, it is more a hymn of praise than a description, and not only because the toiler who is the hero of the book is a hero indeed – a figure, in his humanity, simplicity, worthy of inclusion in the catalogue of mythical giants alongside Hercules, Atlas, Gargantua and Orion. He is Faussone, a rigger'
**Bernard Levin** *The Times*

0 349 10012 8
FICTION